MAN OF FIRE

MAN OF FIRE

Father Emmanuel d'Alzon and the
Oblates of the Assumption.

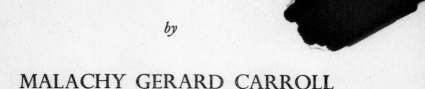

by

MALACHY GERARD CARROLL

With a Foreword by
HIS LORDSHIP THE BISHOP OF BRENTWOOD

MCMLV
THE MERCIER PRESS LIMITED
CORK

First published in October, 1955, by
THE MERCIER PRESS LIMITED
CORK, IRELAND

Nihil Obstat : DERMITIUS FOGARTY, S.T.D.,
Censor Deputatus.

Imprimatur :   H. GIBNEY, V.G.

Southwarci, die 19a, Augusti, 1955.

In conformity with the decree of Pope Urban VIII, the author declares that all which is written in this book is based only on the certitude of human testimony. Every supernatural manifestation recorded in these pages is submitted to the judgment of the Church.

Printed in Great Britain
at the BURLEIGH PRESS, *Lewins Mead,* BRISTOL

CONTENTS

" I no longer belong to myself, but I am in the hands of my Spouse as an instrument on which He Himself plays and from which He plucks canticles to proclaim His Mercy and my love."

EMMANUEL D'ALZON.

" Life of an Oblate Life of Oblation. "

FR. GERVAIS QUENARD A.A.

FOREWORD

To MOST OF US the expression "the French Revolution" conjures up a picture of the guillotine and tumbrils, of ragged revolutionary troops, of the Scarlet Pimpernel and *A Tale of Two Cities*. Historians see it as a turning-point in European history and the beginning of a new age, often confusingly spoken of as the age of liberalism or democracy.

Few people who think along these lines have any clear idea of the principles which inspired the revolution or what its theory really implied. The Declaration of the Rights of Man and of the Citizen of 1789 is rarely read and surprisingly seldom finds its way into history text-books. Many of the articles in that declaration are now taken for granted and this perhaps more than anything else shows how far western society has moved from its Christian origins. "The principle of all sovereignty resides essentially in the nation", and "Law is the expression of the general will", are two examples of the naturalism at the core of so much eighteenth-century thought, which inspired the revolution and which has done so much to fashion the modern mind.

To Emmanuel d'Alzon the "spirit of the Revolution" was a living blasphemy. It was the deliberate denial of God and of His rights in social and public life. He saw it as the source of most of the evils which to-day afflict our world. Inspired with a virile and passionate love of God, he dedicated his whole active life, lived as it was at full pressure, to combating that spirit, and claiming for God His due place in the affairs of men.

To-day we witness the growing disintegration which Father d'Alzon foresaw so clearly. Western civilisation is living on a dwindling capital of Christian and Catholic tradition which is rapidly running dry. Sir Richard Livingstone, himself a defender of the classics, saw only too clearly the end to which it might lead. The following passage from *Education for a World Adrift*

I

presents his case : " We have inherited good habits, and habits persist almost indefinitely if there is nothing to destroy them. A plant may continue in apparent health for some time after its roots have been cut, yet its days are numbered. The case of Germany witnesses to the truth of this contention. Who, thirty years ago, would have believed a prophet who said that a decent, friendly, highly educated and civilised people, among whom Christianity was apparently still strong, would be capable of the persecution of the Jews, the horrors of the concentration camps, the barbarism, knowing neither justice nor mercy nor truth, shown in so many lands ? How astonishing, we say, that such things could happen in the twentieth century ! It is not in the least astonishing. The spiritual roots of Germany had been cut, and rootless virtues are precarious. But how strong are the roots of *our* virtues ? The philosophy of life, the standards by which the Victorian and earlier ages were governed, have broken down. We are left with traditions and habits of conduct inherited from them, as the earth may for a time still receive light from an extinct star. But that light will not continue to shine, nor can these habits and traditions long survive the beliefs from which they grew. Those who reject Christian beliefs cannot count on keeping Christian morals."

Emmanuel d'Alzon left to his successors, whether to the Assumptionist Fathers or to the Oblate Sisters, a legacy under three heads by which he hoped to stem the tide of naturalism. His religious were to fight for sound teaching according to the principles of St. Augustine and St. Thomas Aquinas. They were to fight for a sound social order by waging war against the " spirit of the Revolution ". And they were to be defenders always of the unity of the Church of Christ.

In the following vivid pages, Mr. Carroll has recaptured the sweeping zeal of the great fight of Emmanuel d'Alzon and has helped us to understand something of the spirit that inspired him. He was one of a remarkable group of French Catholics of whom Dom Guéranger, Père Lacordaire and Montalembert are probably best remembered. In some ways we may feel that the Catholic revival which they inspired has tended to flicker out and to dissipate itself. To-day more than ever we need

FOREWORD

their spirit. Perhaps this book may do something to rekindle in our midst the zeal for Christ, for His Church and for His Mother, which produced such fruits in the life of Father d'Alzon and his immediate followers.

✠ GEORGE ANDREW BECK, A.A.

Bishop of Brentwood.

LETTER OF RECOMMENDATION

THE OFFICIALS of the Congregation of Rites in Rome said of Emmanuel d'Alzon : " E un gigante ". " He is a giant ". Father d'Alzon was indeed a powerful and lofty soul, a staunch defender of the Church, a fiery apostle and a saintly priest. His devouring zeal was remarkably versatile. While being the active Vicar General of his diocese, he directed a college in a new and bold spirit, he led the French Catholics' fight for freedom of education, he founded a Carmel, an orphanage, a society praying for Catholic unity, and so on. Above all, however, his name lives on as that of a religious founder.

Not long after their foundation by Father d'Alzon, the Augustinians of the Assumption were sent, at the request of Pope Pius IX to be missionaries in Bulgaria and Turkey. It soon became obvious that women were needed to help by doing such work as teaching the children and the girls, and nursing the sick. To fill that need, Father d'Alzon founded the Oblates of the Assumption. Later, they helped the Assumptionists in other fields, particularly in the apostolate of the press ; then, little by little, they took over hospitals, schools and other institutions. And so the Oblates became distinguished not so much by a definite and limited form of apostolic endeavour as by their spirit.

Father d'Alzon instilled into the minds and hearts of the Oblates the characteristics of his own interior life : a deep and vivid faith, a burning love for Christ, for His Mother and for His Church. The triple love is the only incentive which gave the Oblates the courage and enthusiasm necessary to face every challenge, to be ready for any task, to be prompt and efficient in the service of the Master. They were trained to be generous ; they consider themselves " expendable ".

Thus they have spent themselves, generation after generation, for nearly a century. Malachy Carroll praises in a special way the exceptional virtue of these hidden souls whose duty it was to serve in a multiplicity of tasks, and who served faithfully, despite the drudgery of monotonous repetition. Their heroism went unsuspected by the world. Nevertheless they served, and gave invaluable assistance to the apostolate of the Fathers. God alone knows the multitude of souls that will be credited to them. Their presence at the Bonne Presse in Paris deserves special mention; not only have they rendered this great institution possible by assisting in the work since its inception, but they preserved its very existence during a period of persecution when there were but two Fathers left there. There are Oblates in England, in the Low Countries, in Africa and soon they will be in America. There are Oblates beyond the Iron Curtain, members of the Church of Silence. Everywhere they seek to fulfil the Lord's wishes. "Here am I, send me!"

Vocations are generally reported to be on the wane. A vocation is a calling. Someone has aptly pointed out that vocations in that sense cannot be said to be lacking; in other words, it cannot be believed that God does not beckon enough souls to a life of perfection and dedication to His cause. Obviously, what is missing is the will to comply with the divine invitation. Young men and young women are too often wanting in generosity; they are not in the habit of self-denial. Nor do they effectively believe that God rewards His friends a hundredfold. Hence they deprive Him of a temporal glory, and they deprive themselves of what could be a genuinely happy life, a life that could be a thousand times more fruitful for the Kingdom of Christ.

I pray that this book may induce many young women to answer the call.

WILFRID J. DUFAULT, A.A.
Superior General.

ROME,
OUR LADY OF SORROWS.
April 1,
1955.

YOUTH AND INHERITANCE

THERE IS A RHYTHM in nature, the rhythm of birth and maturity and peaceful age. But there are men who step into the great highway of life with great, purposeful strides and with flashing eyes aglow; they fling the name of Christ burningly in the sky before them, and their eyes are never lowered from Its tremendous challenge; they are men in a hurry, hungry for grace, whose years are crowded years; and yet, when the evening of life comes for them, the fine rapture of their dawn is still with them in all the freshness of its dew and its bird-call. The word *rest* is not in their vocabulary, and they have struck out the word *cannot*. Their spirit stands up straight with the same courage to meet the same challenge of the God-Man whose *Learn of Me* has echoed in the arches of the years. The wonder of grace is the miracle of eternal life, for there are no wrinkles of decay in the spirit of man except those put there by sin. It is good, therefore, to reverse the order of his years, and to see the autumnal splendour of such a man as Emmanuel d'Alzon, before turning to his beginnings and to the heaped-up achievements of his years.

The year is 1875, and Emmanuel d'Alzon is sixty-five years old. He has reached the age when men step back from the fever and the struggle, and are glad to crown a life of labour with the few years of ease that slope them gently towards the grave. Measured in achievement, there are six men in this Emmanuel d'Alzon, and in his years are splendours sufficient to crown all six. Yet he does not rest. Evening has come after a busy day; and to-morrow's toil waits for him when he steps over the threshold of the silence of his prayer. Now he is alone, sitting at his table, pen in hand. Some sheets of paper have already been covered with his headlong handwriting. Now and then he looks up, and a variety of expressions crosses his face. Sometimes the corners of the eyes are wrinkled with delightful humour, and he writes quickly; sometimes you notice a hint of irony in the humour, and you suspect a little caustic touch in the words written; and sometimes the face is grave and thoughtful, and there is a long silent pause before the words are written. It is impossible not to tiptoe forward and read over his shoulder. The eavesdropping is rewarded, for here, in his own handwriting, unconsciously traced in one beautiful nervous passage, are the spiritual lines of the man Emmanuel d'Alzon.

The paper is headed: *Memoir of an Old Boy.* You read the first lines of delicious banter: "*Who am I? What concern is that of yours, my friend? My concern is to be a faithful narrator of events—and believe me, if I bore you, do you think it will give me pleasure to see you yawning at the very sight of my name? . . . Anyhow, it is said that one Father d'Alzon—a man who came into the world with a minimum dose of originality—had the idea. . . .*" You read quickly on, and there are many smiles, many times when you catch your breath with pleasure at the crisp neatness of a phrase, the few words that bring a companion to life as with the stroke of a pencil, and then you come in amazement on the passage that lays bare the mighty soul of the writer and shows you the springs of its power:

"*The big soul seeks to see things in themselves; the little soul sees them in relation to itself, no matter what may be the cause. . . . The big soul devotes itself to a cause; the little soul devotes itself to itself, no matter what may be the cause. The big soul lifts itself to hover on the heights; while the little soul, mole-like, hollows out its hole and is quite content to shelter there. For the essential aim of the little soul is to avoid compromising itself, and it calls this prudence. . . . The big soul is absolutely useless without a strong and generous character, for it sees what is to be done but does nothing. . . .*"

Yes, you murmur as you tiptoe away leaving this old man to his thoughts and his burning words, here indeed is the quintessential d'Alzon—the man who flung out the magnificent challenge in the prime of his years: "*We are accused of compromising ourselves. Well, that is our glory. You who call yourselves prudent, I suppose you would have thought Christ Himself rash when*

He compromised His Church by dying on the Cross. . . ." They are no mere words : they pulsate with the power of that 'broad spirit' which was supremely his, and with the strength and the generosity without which such broadness, as he himself implies, would be arid vision without quickening fervour. They are pointed words, too, barbed with irony ; for this man whose spirit was flung wide to all that is great and noble, had a sharp-edged tongue and an acid pen for everything that smacked of smugness, hypocrisy and the sloth that masquerades as prudence. It was inevitable that such a man should bark his knuckles till they bled, against the solid wall of so-called ' common sense ', and then these words would come ; it was inevitable that his ' broad spirit' should beat its luminous wings in something like scorn—or as near to scorn as sanctity will permit—when it hears the little spirit raising its voice of sloth in a cry of prudence ; but the voice of that large spirit can also speak words soft as summer rain that are as balm to struggling souls. Christ too could hurl His sharp words about "white sepulchres", and speak His soft words to the Magdalen. On the threshold of this study of Father d'Alzon, it is good to point the parallel.

From this picture of vigorous old age, we turn to seek back through the years for the child who, in Wordsworth's fine phrase, was ' father of the man '. " A child ", wrote John Earle in one of his essays, " is a man in small letter." In his maturity and in his vigorous age, the qualities that made the greatness of Emmanuel d'Alzon were written in great block letters on his years. We find those same qualities ' in small letter ' in the child Emmanuel d'Alzon, and each letter is written with character and force. He was born at Le Vigan in the Midi of France on August 30th, 1810. His father was the Vicomte Henri Daudé d'Alzon, of highest aristocratic rank. His mother was a commanding woman who could speak a sentence that had the crack of a whip in it, but whose warmth of charity the poor knew and blessed. He was the eldest child, and he had two sisters Augustine and Marie. Many years later, one of his most energetic disciples—the journalist of the Assumption, Father Vincent de Paul Bailly—was to say magnificently that the first school bench of a child is the arm of its mother. A child's home is its first world, and the greater world awaiting it may well be shaped to the image of that first world. We have a fine description of the first world of the child Emmanuel d'Alzon from the contemporary pen of M. de Pontmartin. Speaking of the atmosphere in the fine Château of Lavagnac, to which the d'Alzons moved when Emmanuel was yet a child, he writes : " That hospitable and charming home, over whose threshold never passed a vulgar thought, a mean sentiment, a cold calculation, a frivolous idea, or an empty phrase of worldly egotism." This, as we shall see, is no laudatory orchid handed with a flourish of compliment ; every word is literal truth. We have listed these things briefly, for each had its place in the shaping of Emmanuel d'Alzon towards greatness. But especially must we notice the great sweep of splendour that came to him with the very name *d'Alzon*.

It is a splendid ancestry : the sword shines there, always drawn to defend the right, and the path is red with blood given for the Church. There is the blood of Jean Daudé de la Coste, direct ancestor, who died in defence of the Church in 1580 ; there is the blood of his son and grandson in the next century— and perhaps in that grandson we have a picture of how his descendant Emmanuel d'Alzon might have borne himself, had he followed his first inclination and taken the career of arms. For there is a magnificent moment in the life of Jacques Daudé de la Coste (1687) when, at the head of fifteen dragoons, he routed a force many times greater, with the cry of the Catholic Faith on his lips. The more one studies the life of Emmanuel d'Alzon, the more one realizes what a sweep of courageous qualities came to meet the moment of his birth from that splendid line. Interpreting the symbolism of the d'Alzon crest, Father Picard lists those qualities : " The gold of charity, the strength of a lion, the warrior's courage, the purity of the lily, and above all the giving of self to God and to His Church—such was the family, such was Emmanuel d'Alzon." (*Notes et Documents*, 1. 17.) Weak-kneed creatures have been born to an inheritance of crowded courage, and that inheritance has sunk into the clay beside them because they were not big enough to receive it.

But the spirit of Emmanuel d'Alzon was measured to that fine inheritance, for in him it was to end in a blaze of glory.

The first great formative influence, as with every man, was of course his parents. He was by no means an easy child. "*When I was a little boy*", he wrote, "*I was unendurable—a real thorny stick.*" It was inevitable that there should have been something like fierce energy of spirit in the child, when the man was destined to wield the power of six men ; but Providence provided him with parents whose contrasted characters were splendidly suited to guide him.

Our first glimpse of M. Henri d'Alzon is the moment when the news was brought to him that the son of his prayer had been given to him. He greeted the news with the words : " Blessed is he that cometh in the name of the Lord." Some days later, when he brought that son into the Church at le Vigan—it is one of those venerable churches where every stone seems to pray—the child was christened Emmanuel-Joseph-Marie-Maurice. It is good to find the name Maurice here—for he was the leader of the intrepid and glorious Theban Legion. But it is the name Emmanuel—" God with Us "—that comes as a ray of prophetic light. The motto on the d'Alzon arms was : " Deo dati "— " Given to God." In the very name selected for that child, there was a presage that God would claim from the last of the great line, a literal incarnation of the words on that proud escutcheon. The name *Mary*, too, was happily spoken over this child who, in the name of Mary's Assumption, was to give a new family—indeed, five new families—of spiritual sons and daughters to the Church. " More balanced and more silent than Madame d'Alzon," wrote one of his closest friends, " M d'Alzon seemed to *pontificate* in his own home. Yet, this stern Christian showed all the tenderness of paternal love and all the delicacy of Christian charity." He was also a man of a delicacy of conscience which verged on the scrupulous—a fact which may well explain why in youth he set his foot on the way to the priesthood, but decided otherwise. The life of a priest with a hyper-sensitive conscience like that of Henri d'Alzon would be a continual agony. The Parish-Priest who served Lavagnac heard the confession of M. d'Alzon a moment before Mass in order that the Comte might receive communion with an easy mind : it is clear that, had M. d'Alzon become Father d'Alzon, he would have required a confessor-in-ordinary at his elbow at any moment of the day and night when he had to perform any of his sacred duties. It was an excellent thing that his son did not inherit that trait, for it could certainly have ruined his work. His father had all the finest qualities of a Christian gentleman, and these he passed on to his son. These qualities had been tried in the maelstrom of the Revolution, when " France got drunk with blood to vomit crime " ; and the young Henri had kept himself unspotted from it all. Emmanuel's father might possibly be criticized as one who gave the impression of tiptoeing on the Ten Commandments as though they were made of glass ; but the important fact for the life story of Emmanuel is that from his earliest years he had before him an example of a passionate love for purity and uprightness. " *I do not believe*," wrote Emmanuel many years later, " *that my father was ever guilty of a deliberate venial sin.*" Another important factor is that this father was a man of literary culture, possessed of that sensitive receptivity to the beautiful which has been called the sanctity of the intellect. When one glances to-day over the library of Father Emmanuel d'Alzon, as it is carefully preserved in his fine college at Nîmes, it is clear that the fine intellectual heritage of sweetness and light passed on to the son. It combined splendidly with his other heritage—the heritage from his mother.

Turning again to the contemporary accounts, we find a vivid sentence which sets in focus the contrasted relations of father and son, and of mother and son. " While M. d'Alzon looked silently at his son, rejoicing in him, Madame d'Alzon used to *devour him*." In comparison with the deep silent waters of her husband's spirit, she was as a rushing river, or even a cataract. She was a woman of spirit and fire, whose one fault seems to have been that she could ill brook contradiction. Madame d'Alzon was an aristocrat, and she never allowed herself to forget the *noblesse oblige* which this demanded, nor anyone else to step beyond the limits of familiarity set by her. If a person did so, a few precise words cut the air like a whip, and the presumptuous one stepped back hurriedly over the line of decorum that should not have been crossed. Only then would Madame revert to her habitual attitude of cultured courtesy. Madame had bred a son of this same stamp, and it was because she recognized this spirit that she used *to devour* him, as the writer said. But there are the flints of friction in such similarity, and from the very outset we feel that there will be moments when the clash of temperaments will bring some sparks of passing discord. And yet, Emmanuel d'Alzon is the first to admit that the greatest formative influence on his life was his mother. She gave him a temperament that swept him into the adventure of living with a magnificent enthusiasm.

" This fine Christian lady ", we are told, " had put her Lavagnac château on a footing of princely distinction, which impressed all her guests and singularly enhanced the prestige of her children. Yet a remarkable simplicity went with this stamp of dignity and grandeur." One feels that she thought of Emmanuel's fitting into all this, as it were a nimbus of aristocratic splendour circling his own splendour. Poor lady, her dream was to have a rude awakening, even if eventually a glorious one. Her son had been born into greatness and riches. The window of the room at Le Vigan where he was born, looked out over d'Alzon land to where a d'Alzon hill lifted itself heavy with its rich vines. But the heir to all its glory would sell it all and scatter it in the wild enthusiasm of his cry—*Adveniat Regnum Tuum*; in vain did she build up the splendour of Lavagnac for him, with its extensive lands, its fine château reflected in the calm waters of a lake— for he was to step out of the nimbus and bury himself in a foul street in Nîmes. This street, more than anything else, brings home to the searcher for the living d'Alzon, the immense catastrophe—in the eyes of his mother—of his betrayal of all the glory she had dreamed for him. It is a street—this *rue de l'Arc du Gras*—so narrow that you can almost span it with outstretched arms, and it must certainly be the meanest in Nîmes. She visited her son there on foot, for the streets narrowed too much to allow her carriage to pass. One imagines how she must have stepped daintily along that rough street, avoiding the mud, and lamenting with some bitterness this headstrong conduct of her son. But woe to the person who dared to join with her in censuring him, as the good lady learnt to her cost who presumed to condone with her on the charitable extravagances of her son. "Madame," came the reply in words as dry and as sharp as splinters of glass, "if my son had scattered all that money in riot and debauchery, you would smile indulgently and say nothing! It is for God, and of course that trips yon up! Know, Madame, that this is a glory!..." The whip had been cracked, and Madame knew she had been indiscreet.

As the eldest, Emmanuel took a great interest in the welfare of his two sisters, Augustine and Marie—but it was to Augustine that he was most attached. "There was in this young girl", reads the contemporary account of M. de Pontmartin, "the stuff of a Eugénie de Guérin, or of one of those delicate creatures who live again in the *Diary of a Sister*." Perhaps we may indeed grant the same delicacy of character-outline; but there must be no hint that Augustine could possibly have attached herself to her brother with the neurotic fervour of the girl who wrote: *Mon âme ne coule de pente que dans ton âme.* There was nothing of Maurice de Guérin in Maurice d'Alzon either. The contemporary accounts emphasize Augustine's great purity, her sweet saintly look—in fact, there is such a blaze of white in the account that it is hard to fix the human lines, as in those old lives of the saints when the saint is swallowed up in the halo. There is one significant sentence in M. de Pontmartin's vignette of her, however: "Every so often she would say something in which the angel would give place to the woman." That is better! M. de Pontmartin gives one of her mildly ironical remarks, and one wishes he had given more. It would be possible to present her as the gentle white angel of the d'Alzon household: "in softened colours, delicate tones and a great delicacy of brushwork, those same qualities are found in her which have been used to present the characters of the others in bold lines and dramatic colouring." It seems more to the point to emphasize the magnificent strength of character and of will that this young girl must have had, to efface herself so carefully in the service of her parents. Emmanuel chose the priesthood; Marie became la Comtesse de Puységur; Augustine, with as clearly defined a vocation for the religious life as a girl could have, buried it deep in her because her father and mother needed her. It bore a splendid harvest of charity for the country folk on the d'Alzon estates. Madame d'Alzon was very charitable, but one feels that a certain hauteur went with the dispensing ; her daughter's charity had a kneeling humility in it. Even allowing for an old lady's simple enthusiasm, this is a magnificent tribute from one who knew her : " For thirty-five years ", writes this woman of Saint-Pons, " I have thought only of God and of Mlle. Augustine. When she came, it seemed as if the Blessed Virgin herself entered the house. She was so good, so humble. She would take the lowliest place, or even sit on the floor. . . . She would teach us the Catechism. . . . She would not accept even a glass of water—she who distributed so much alms ! . . ." A priest friend of the family completes the picture : " Mlle. Augustine would dress the wounds of the poor, sweep their rooms, perform the most humble, the most simple, the most generous offices of charity. She was a saint ! " She wore herself away to an early death in the service of her parents and her poor; her lungs were exhausted, we are told, from reading in a very loud voice to her aged and semi-deaf father. And she died with a gesture of beauty, of delicacy, of heroism that seems to lift all the secret greatness of her soul into a final moment of blinding splendour. We give it in the simple and moving words of Father Picard :

" The day of her death was her Father's birthday. She had the courage to surmount the anguish of her last agony, to prepare and send a bouquet to her father. It withered, and he treasured it as a relic."

We have gone forward into the years to finish this portrait of Augustine. The courage of her life, the courage with which she faced an early death, was a magnificent example to her brother of the power that lives in humility and self-effacement. But her life was something more wonderful still. As one reaches through the years to fix the lines of Augustine's life, another shadowy figure seems to hover indistinctly beside her as though she were shadowing forth something in the future. One gradually recognizes that figure—that gentle step coming quietly, that taking of the lowest place, that humble ministering

to the sick, that busy brush sweeping the poor man's room. . . .
Yes, it is no fancy to say that Augustine foreshadowed the Little
Sister of the Assumption whose place to-day—to the glory of
the gentle Etienne Pernet, spiritual son of Emmanuel d'Alzon—
is in the throbbing heart of the great Assumptionist ideal.
When Father d'Alzon—their ' grandfather ' as they affectionately
called him—visited the ' Little Sisters ', the spiritual ' cousins' of
the Oblates, did he ever look at them and see the gentle figure
of his sister take her place in spirit among them ?

Let us complete the family album by following Marie into
her years. She was a sensitive and courageous girl who enjoyed
the roses of life but did not shrink from its thorns. In a passage
of delicately woven thought, she writes to her father : " At
first I saw only the roses, but my thoughts led me to glimpse
the thorns and at the same time to accept them, according to God's
will for me. I pray Him to call me to Himself, rather than allow
me to act so as to displease Him. . . ." The thorns she glimpsed
were very soon painfully with her. In the rose bloom of her
married bliss, her husband was struck down with a sickness that
soon proved fatal. Her brother—Father Emmanuel—was there
to comfort her during her husband's last illness. Even before
this, a thorn of particular keenness had pierced her soul. She
had taken her little daughter of five to visit the chapel of the
family château. The child carried a bouquet of flowers to place
at Our Lady's feet. It was Mary's month of May, and Marie
Comtesse de Puységur was sending her little one to offer her
flowers. But it pleased the Mother of God to ask the gift of her
child. The little one was running eagerly up the steps when she
was seized with a heart attack which soon carried her innocent
soul to Mary's feet. It is strange that a bouquet of flowers
should again figure in the d'Alzon story. It was a terrible blow,
but Marie bore it with fortitude and resignation, just as she was
later to bear the separation from her eldest daughter who, in
Father Picard's lovely phrase, left her " to bury her beauty
under the veil of penance " in Notre-Dame du Mont Carmel.
" What more could she give ? " asks Father Picard. And he
continues :

" She had given all : she now gave herself. In spite of these searing sorrows, she is found consoling, loving, sustaining her friends, and showing to all the straight way of duty. She is found continuing the traditions of her family, visiting and comforting the poor, imposing secret privations on herself to increase the bounty of her alms, leading a life of extreme simplicity."

It would be difficult to improve on Father Picard's description of the death of this magnificent Christian lady:

" Against the laws of all human probability, this valiant woman —the pride and joy of Father d'Alzon—died in Nîmes under his very eyes. No words could describe the faith, the simple and moving beauty of those last conversations between brother and sister. She made her Confession to him. It pleased God that he who had opened to her the ways of holiness, should have the consolation of opening to her the kingdom of Heaven."

It is worth while to lay down in its entirety at the beginning of the life of Emmanuel d'Alzon, what might be called *the d'Alzon pattern*. We have gone forward in the years to complete that pattern as shown in the life stories of Augustine and Marie. It is a pattern of forthrightness, of courage, of a great strength and an immense gentleness. Each of them realized that pattern in her life after her own fashion ; and it came to splendid achievement, to a realization throbbingly alive, in the life of their brother.

There are perhaps three moments which are worth recapturing in the childhood of Emmanuel d'Alzon, because they show the forthright character that will develop with the years. The first catches him as little more than a baby, sitting at table with two governesses—one to fill a spoon while the other administered a spoonful. " He was no Pantagruel nor more of a glutton than another," says Vailhé; " it was simply that he was in a hurry to leave the table—and he was in the same hurry all his life." The picture is completed by a glimpse we catch of a little boy who, with all the eagerness of a healthy appetite, rushed to the table to hurl himself on whatever dainties remained over. " The servant ", we are told, " arrived in time to save a little of the dessert ! " We find him later, as a student, curbing this tendency to gluttony and to the headlong. "*I am naturally a gourmand,*" he wrote to Mère Eugénie de Jesus. "*I hit on the plan of buying a bag of highly perfumed and wholly delicious chocolate bon-bons, and leaving them on my desk. From time to time, I felt their temptation and I said to myself : 'You shall not touch them.'*" There is no merit in the impatient, the headlong, the reckless ; but when a man is endowed by nature with verve and with drive, and yet learns early to use the snaffle and the curb, he becomes a great man. The holiness of Emmanuel d'Alzon is stamped with immense energy of spirit, but its secret is that he was always in control. The horse never ran away with its rider.

The second incident shows the determination and the ready answer which were to characterize him always. Some of the *grandes dames* of the neighbourhood were visiting Lavagnac, and they asked to see the little, seven-year-old Emmanuel. A game was in full swing, and he did not appreciate in the least being interrupted. It was therefore a very stubborn little boy, with fists tightly clenched behind his back, who came in to the ladies. His mother ordered him to salute the visitors. He looked about him, and grinned as he noticed some Protestants among them. Still proudly erect, he said in a loud, clear voice : " Outside the Church—*pas de salut* ! "* The sally was greeted with laughter, and the whole incident ended in triumph for him. It was abundantly clear from the outset that Emmanuel d'Alzon would never be at a loss for an answer.

Among the children, he was the energetic hub of every game. When he got himself into a scrape, and was punished by being imprisoned alone among the dining-room chairs, a delegate was sure to arrive from the children for him—because the game had fallen flat without him. " Swift and vigorous, full of sap," writes Vailhé, " he would run with the agility of an antelope, climbing obstacles, jumping terraces and borders of garden and of park as if they were steps of stairs, clambering in trees and revealing his presence there only by the tricks he played on those passing underneath." It is a picture of great verve and energy—and there is a mother's strong hand and a salutory

* . . . there is no salvation !

switch in the background to keep it all within due limits ! A
tutor was engaged for him, and Emmanuel was to speak later
in somewhat disparaging tones of " the hothouse education I
received." Even as a child, he made an amusing protest against
it. He liked to play liturgical games, and once, at the age of
twelve, we find him celebrating a marriage. His usual audience
for such pious exploits was swollen by members of the household, among whom was his tutor. The time came for the
exhortation to the bride and bridegroom. With a mock
seriousness in his voice, and a sly look at the grown-ups,
he said : " My dear friends, if the good God blesses you with
children, do not hand them over to a tutor, but bring them up
yourselves ! "

There are, however, one or two other incidents that must be
noticed, if this picture of swiftness is not to be one-sided. There
is, for example, the little boy who was found standing perfectly
still on tip-toe, looking through the keyhole of the locked
oratory door ; who, when asked what he is doing, says simply
" I am adoring." In the great, energetic forward-sweep of
Emmanuel d'Alzon's life, there will always be a point of calm
in the centre of his being where he is speaking with his God.
. . . Leaving this little boy on tiptoe, and going forward into his
years, we find that same " I am adoring " as the secret of all.
" One day—it must have been in 1859," writes Canon Galeran
(*Croquis*), " Father d'Alzon stopped off at my house in Montpellier. He seemed tired, depressed, preoccupied. ' My friend,'
he said to me, ' I have stopped here because I have a serious
matter to discuss with Our Lord. I shall go into your chapel,
behind the altar. I need nothing, and please leave me absolutely
alone.' On entering the chapel, he prostrated himself at the
foot of the altar, his face to the ground. . . . In an hour and a
half, he came to me again. He was changed. His face wore
an expression of joy, and his eyes were still wet with the tears
he must have shed. . . ." Some years previous to this incident,
when the news came that Emmanuel d'Alzon was thinking of
becoming a Carthusian, a friend of his said : " What ! D'Alzon
a monk ! A steam-engine in a cell ! " It was a witty and a
wise comment, for Emmanuel would never have made a

Carthusian ; but if we are to accept the metaphor of the steam-engine, it must be of one where the driving force is the white heat of contemplation.   Side by side in the heart of the young Emmanuel, were the boy who dashed recklessly on horseback, all caution thrown to the winds ; the boy who played at saying Mass, chanting the Passion with an empty barrel as his rostrum, and who could be punished beyond all the powers of tongue or of switch merely by being denied the privilege of attending Vespers ; the boy who rushed forward to meet the poor, that he might give and give ; the boy who impetuously put his arm in the fire, and bore the mark to his grave, in order that he might know what Purgatory was like and learn a greater sympathy.   All these were to grow, to mellow, and to merge into the character of the man whose whole energy would be impregnated with what Jefferies called " the furnace-like vehemence of prayer."

Finally, it is with a shock of pleasure that we meet in the boy d'Alzon the germ of d'Alzon the Father Confessor.   We give the incident as reported in *Notes et Documents* : " On the eve of a certain feast," relates his cousin, " I said to his sister Augustine as we walked together in the court of the château : ' I cannot go to Holy Communion to-morrow because I have something on my mind which troubles me.'—' Tell Emmanuel about it,' she promptly answered.—' No,' I remonstrated, ' you are joking.'—' I assure you he will set your mind at rest.   He is excellent at doing that ! '—and seeing him in the distance, she called him, told him he must give me some advice, and left us alone.   He became very serious, and I told him what was on my mind.   He dismissed it as unimportant, and assured me that I could go to the good God, which indeed I did the next morning, very reassured and very tranquil. . . ."

It is with this little tableau of his gentleness, his understanding, and the confidence he could inspire, that we leave the childhood of Emmanuel d'Alzon.   He had been placed in the rich soil of the d'Alzon tradition, and like the vigorous young plant that he was, he had sent his roots down deep to gather to himself all that was most noble and most energetic and most nobly simple, sincere and gentle in that centuries-old loam. Men were to call him " the lion of the Cévennes "—but in the heart of that lion were the humility and gentleness of a lamb. The lion and the lamb lay down together in the years of Emmanuel d'Alzon

EMMANUEL D'ALZON STUDENT

IN MAY, 1822, Vicomte d'Alzon was elected *député de l'Herault* and in October of the following year his family joined him in the hôtel Crapelet, rue de Vaugirard, near Saint-Sulpice in Paris. The thirteen years of what he called " his hothouse upbringing " at Lavagnac were over, and he turned the leaf to find a new page of life blank before him, headed with the word " Adolescence "—a word which carries in its turbulent heart all the storm and the stress, the grand enthusiasms and the big generosities of youth, the dangers and the pitfalls. But there was another word written on that page—the word " First Holy Communion " which Emmanuel received in December, 1824. It is no fancy to look ahead over those years which began with his schooling in Saint-Louis and ended with his entry into the Seminary of Montpellier, and to see them white with the reflected whiteness of the Host, pure with the purity that comes from living always with the remembrance of Mary's purity. His mother and father had fostered a love for purity in him, and now that love was to become a passion, reaching to the innermost recesses of his being to become the secret strength of all his achievements. He received the Sacrament of Confirmation eight days after his first Communion, and the mark of " strong and perfect Christian " which comes with that Sacrament was to be something real and living in the years of Emmanuel d'Alzon.

It is too easy to pass over the adolescent years of a young man of God as though their spotlessness were something effortless, as though he had been born to a purity which grew with him as naturally as his bodily growth. Purity of such a negative kind would be indicative of spiritual lethargy in a man, a clear indication that he was lacking in the vital energy needed to become a great saint—or even a great sinner. Christian purity is vital, is dynamic, is supremely positive, and it is the fruit of vigilance and of prayer. Purity is spiritual power, and it was that power that went out from Emmanuel d'Alzon to all who came in contact with him at every stage of his life. But he had to struggle to preserve it in those impressionable years. This was indeed as it should be; for the man who cannot experience human feelings will lack that fundamental contact with human nature which is so necessary to a good priest. Yes, Emmanuel d'Alzon had the purity of an angel—and the rich, warm blood of a man.

Passing over the early student years, we come to that vital moment when Emmanuel stood at the gate of life, wondering which way he should take. He had developed a passion for reading and study, and his father had been as a vigilant angel of guidance to him in selecting what he should read. These 'letters to a son' are models of how an intelligent and eager youth should be encouraged, stimulated, guided in his reading, not just snuffed out with an omniscient ' don't-read-it '. Does he wish his son to avoid Montesquieu's *Esprit des lois*? He offers him an alternative: " You can therefore run after quite another hare. I would rather see you reading Fernand's *Esprit de l'histoire* . . ." There is question of Pascal: " You would be well advised to buy Pascal's *Pensées*, but ignore the notes which are very pernicious. They are Voltaire's notes even though under another's name . . ." Thus, fine, constructive criticism and guidance came to the student at the College Stanislas from his father about many books and many topics. It must have been a great joy to such a father to have this link of intellectual intimacy with his son. The fruit of all this was the balanced and sensitive mind of Emmanuel d'Alzon to all that is finest in thought and expression. There was seething intellectual energy in this son of his, and a man as intelligent as Henri Daudé d'Alzon must have divined in this youth the man who would ' splash at a ten-league canvas ' to feed that energy; it was good, therefore, that the curb of Christian prudence should be there from the outset.

We shall have ample evidence of how well Emmanuel became stained through with this literary culture when we come to examine his letter on Christian friendship, his most significant writing from this period. But it is worth while to isolate here a letter on literature which he wrote at the end of this period when he was twenty-one :

"*I maintain, in spite of what* L'Avenir *and even the* Correspondant *may say, that the perfection of literature is not romanticism, is not Sainte-Beuve any more than it is Victor Hugo. There is a deep meaning which has not been understood, a chord which has not been plucked. My dear friend, you have the Faith, you who believe what you say, do you not feel within you something which is not expressed by anyone in modern literature? I mean, in poetry, that evangelical high seriousness which La Bruyère found in the Christian orators. I have found some traces of it in Dante, in Tasso ; but among our poets, even Lamartine himself has not measured up to the full height of my idea. I believe the reason for this is that, to be a poet, one must have a great natural wealth of sentiment ; but ill-directed sentiment feeds the passions, and hence the poets have too often profaned to impure uses the beauty of the gifts they have received.*"

Again, in writing to his poet-friend, Eugène de la Gournerie, he speaks of "*that kind of chaste beauty*" which alone can inspire great poetry :

"*Your poetry breathes a freshness, a simplicity, a charming candour which is so very rare to-day because our poets are always disillusioned and jaded, knowing evil, doing evil, so that, for all their talent, they will never attain to that kind of chaste beauty which you reach, any more than the cheek of the courtesan can know that blush of modesty which floods the face of a virgin.*"

This is the writing of a young man of twenty-one, and it argues a great richness of reading and of thought in the years since, as a lad of thirteen, he began his studies in Paris. It is studded with evidence of his wide reading, and as we retrace our steps we find books littered everywhere. The whetstone on which he sharpened his mind was composed of an amazing variety of flints : Dante, Tasso, Augustine, Pascal, Scott, Cervantes, Tertullian, Plato, Malebranche, Saint-Simon, Goethe, Byron, Hugo . . . and the list could go on and on. But in spite of all this, there had come a moment in the early adolescence of Emmanuel when the ancestral soldier had stood up in him and pointed the way to the career of arms. For a while, the sword was to hold up its challenge on the horizon of his years, beckoning to the chivalry within him; and then that sword was to fade that the sword of the spirit might take its place, and he would then reach out a consecrated hand to take that mystic sword and to answer a glorious call to arms.

It came as a surprise to his father when, during the vacation of 1826, Emmanuel announced his intention of preparing to enter Saint-Cyr with a view to following a military career. His father had other dreams for him—a place in diplomatic circles, in the administration or the magistracy. When the vacation was over, he appealed to Emmanuel not to change the literary direction of his studies, but to wait till he could come to a more mature decision. There followed an exchange of letters in which the boy seemed to entrench himself more and more in his decision, while his father reasoned and appealed. In a letter of January 19th, 1827, we find him offering to his son the alternative of Saint-Cyr or a library:

" You have two ideas," he writes, " which you keep always foremost in your mind : Saint-Cyr and your library. As to the first, while we would not in the least diminish that trust to which we attach great importance, it seems to your mother and me that, in the interests of your own happiness and of ours, you might speak of your desire to enter Saint-Cyr with a little more consideration for the pain you know it causes us. You have never written in a manner calculated to soften the sacrifice for me, if God really wills that you should follow the military profession. I think you have made as little effort to soften it for your poor mother, for you write to me quite bluntly : ' Mother may grumble, but I still think a lot about Saint-Cyr.' I would be distressed if you were not open with us about what you think and what you wish, and if you were to be the least deceitful in your relations with us ; but I would also like you to show that you are a little more sensible of the distress which your entry into Saint-Cyr will cause us—a distress which is only too justified by our fear of the dangers to which we know you will be exposed, and our knowledge of the long separation which this will cause, both on your entering the School and on your leaving it."

After further reasonings and appeals, he returns to the point which he considers will have greatest influence with his son:

" Your ardent desire to have a library serves only to strengthen the opinion I have of your desire to enter Saint-Cyr. And, I appeal to you, tell me what need will you have for a library if you enter there ? "

It was an anxious time for his father, who did not want to bully his son into shaping his life according to a parent's pattern, but who at the same time realized that there were strong indications in that son that pointed the other way. In a vivid letter of December, 1826, he had expressed his opinion very clearly about this whim of his son's : " It appears, my dear Emmanuel, that the nettle-rash which you have just had, has affected not only your blood but also your imagination. In your previous letters, you showed only pacific and quiet tastes, you dreamed only of the charm and pleasure of having a library . . . But to-day, I know not what fanfare of trumpets has sounded in your ears. Good-bye, books ! . . ."

These extracts give an interesting sidelight on the hard vein of thoughtlessness that can exist in even the best of boys. Life is an adventure, and they turn to meet that adventure, now facing one way with warm enthusiasm, now facing another, and always unconscious of the anxiety of parents who watch it all from the higher places of their experience. The problem for Emmanuel was precisely this : that he would have to discover a vocation in which the sword and the book, the warrior and the student, could be accommodated. One day he would find it ; but for the moment he would allow the library to hold the field, as we see from a letter of his father's in which every word breathes relief:

" It gives me great pleasure," he writes in May, 1827, " to see that you are no longer thinking of Saint-Cyr, and that this does not prevent you from giving yourself to study."

He goes on to underline how much more compatible with his love " for Greek and other literary studies " would be Law. " I assure you that there are persons in the *Conseil d'Etat* whose delight in reading Demosthenes and Bourdaloue has not been diminished by their becoming experts in the interpretation of ordinances and of laws."

So be it—Emmanuel turned to Law. But in spite of the evidence of those literary lawyers who could keep an eagle eye on the Code Napoleon and an æsthetic eye on the splendours of Demosthenes, it must be confessed that literary aspirations in the field of Law are very much like geraniums planted in sawdust, and stand the same chance of survival. Of one thing, however, we can be sure : that he left no doubt in his father's mind about the reality of his conversion to Law. In fact, his enthusiasm had already burned all the rungs of the ladder of legal fame, and he saw himself at the age of forty—the age of eligibility—holding a seat in Parliament! One senses the smile of amusement behind his father's reply :

"My dear Emmanuel, it is perhaps looking a little far ahead to see yourself twenty-three years hence ! "

Someone has spoken of 'the delicious malady of being seventeen.' There are no obstacles behind the horizon when one is seventeen, and about one's feet the dew is on the grass and the glory is in the flower. Emmanuel saw himself blazing a trail through Law, and he did indeed blaze it—for a year or so. By then, he had begun to feel the sawdust in his soul. There are the diagrammatic and the rhythmical minds, as Yeats has told us, and Law calls for the diagrammatic. Emmanuel had the rhythmical type that needs the big horizons and the splendid words for its study. Law can live and rise to glory in a narrow, dusty room, feeding itself with chapter and verse ; Emmanuel could feed on chapter and verse with enthusiasm only when there was a sweep of infinity behind the verse and the chapter. We are not surprised to hear him exclaim after a year's Law : " *Mon Dieu ! how boring this Law is !* " The vision of Emmanuel d'Alzon Deputy to Parliament in 1850 quickly faded. Too much dry dust lay along that road to fame. His literary and philosophical enthusiasm had risen relentlessly as the sea, and what chance had the dutiful little sand-castles of Law-studies against it ? What chance had the *Titres* and *Articles* against the majestic resonance of Bossuet, the subtlety of Lamennais, the limpidity of de Sévigné, the poetry of Augustine ? The hand of God is clear in all this, shaping the destiny of the soldier-student towards something worthy of the 'broad spirit' in him.

The years 1826 to 1828 had been groping years for Emmanuel. He was always conscious of a great fund of energy within him, seeking an outlet and a unity of direction without which it would dissipate itself on a hundred things and achieve nothing. The story of Emmanuel d'Alzon will really begin when he discovers that great unity of purpose which will give meaning to all. At the end of 1828, we meet the first tentative formulation of that master purpose : " *I have discovered my aim*," he writes. " *I wish to consecrate myself entirely to the defence of the Church and of Religion.*" There is a blurred, somewhat indistinct outline about this resolve, but it is a resolve nevertheless and adequate enough for the age of eighteen. A few years will strengthen that outline, will edge the meaning of the words, will bring the gleam of the sword into the resolve, and we will hear those splendid words : " *As a religious, I shall saturate myself with the idea of M. de Rancé and I shall remind myself that a religious must be an angel, a martyr, an apostle.*"

We have followed the life of Emmanuel from his fourteenth to his eighteenth year, through the Collège Saint-Louis to the Collège Saint-Stanislaus, through his few months of determination about Saint-Cyr to his experiment in Law. These are the external things, but behind them and through them is *the* significant feature of this period and of the years which followed—his genius for friendship and his insight into what constituted the essence of Christian friendship. To miss the significance of this in the development of Emmanuel d'Alzon would be to leave a gap in his story. " One day, towards the end of 1830," writes Father Picard (*Notes et Documents*), " he said out of the abundance of his heart to his best friend : ' It would be impossible for me to be an egoist ! ' To which that friend replied : ' Indeed you have the *malady of friendship* . . .' "

' The malady of friendship ' : it is indeed an arresting phrase as one reads the documents and letters from this period of his life. In the period 1827 to 1832, a whole pléiade of men who were later to take eminent places in the world, called him friend. He was a member of the *Société Littéraire*, founded by the eminent M. Bailly, who was to give two of his sons as spiritual sons of d'Alzon in the Assumption ; he was a member of the *Société des Bonnes Etudes*, founded in 1823 ; he also joined the *Association pour la défense de la religion catholique*, which aimed at rallying the forces of the Catholic élite of France. We find his name also among the members of the *Conférence religieuse* who met once a week to study religious or philosophical problems. Through the *Bonnes Etudes*, he came into warm and stimulating contact with Lamennais, whose tragic story we shall study in a later chapter; with M. Combalot, that brilliant and restless man whose work d'Alzon was later to save from shipwreck; with the poet de la Gournerie, to whom he wrote that fine letter on literature we have quoted above . . . " and with a whole pléiade of heroic fighters who were beginning, in face of the ruin heaped up by the Renaissance and the Revolution, the great battle which still continues." Among those he met was Victor Hugo, then a Christian poet, but with pride waiting around the corner to deflect him from his course. It would be interesting to know whether that sentence d'Alzon wrote about the seeds of corruption in the very gift of poetry, was not the result of a close observation of Hugo. We shall have occasion many times to notice the eagle glance of d'Alzon which could get to the essence of a man in a moment.

We are fortunate in having an article on friendship by Emmanuel d'Alzon which shows us what a thing of spotless splendour friendship was to him, and which explains the superlatives used by his friends in describing their relations with him. It is dated June, 1829, and is an absolutely amazing document from a youth of nineteen. He was not concerned with the sentimental trappings of friendship, but, with a thoroughness that was to become second nature to him, he sought for the vivifying first source of Christian friendship. " *He who would discover the first source of a river, would most miserably waste his efforts in digging into the bowels of the earth to find the first gushings of water which unite and finally cover immense space. This is not the right way; there is another and more sure way which has this supreme advantage, that at the end of one's labour there is the fruit. Let him look up to where the clouds overhead are carrying to the mountains the water to feed the springs. And these clouds, whence are they? From an unplumbed ocean, to which all returns, from which all comes, and in which all will be engulfed again. Thus the hidden source is reached. . . . And it is thus with friendship. It is not on earth that one must seek the source from which flows such a wholly divine sentiment. Here too we must look up and see how all friendship has its source in a vast ocean, the First Cause of all our life and of all our affections. We must realize that the nearer we approach that source, by drawing near to Infinite Love, the nearer we are to happiness. For supreme happiness consists in losing ourselves in the immensity of Its depths."*

This is the youth, Emmanuel d'Alzon, thinking out the personal problem of his relations with those he called his friends. The end of his reasoning brings him to God as the ground of all friendship. The masterpiece of love and of friendship is Christ. *" Before Christ,"* he continues, *" what was love, what was friendship ? A mere natural attachment between a man and his fellow man. There was no spiritual exaltation in this friendship and love, of which the Divinity was not the bond. A man and another man— nothing more ; but to-day it is not so. They are two intelligent beings, gifted with the faculty of knowing and of loving, who, to use the language of the poets, marry one another in God."* This thought leads him naturally to Christ's magnificent prayer to His Father for His own, " that they may be one in us."

It was this exalted idea of friendship that he carried alive into his relations with his friends. With such a foundation for friendship, he could keep a rendezvous of the spirit with a friend far from him. " He used to arrange a rendezvous with this friend and with that at the table of Holy Communion," writes Father Picard ; " for Communion was the chosen banquet of those friends who called the Mass the sublime marriage-feast of the soul with Christ." And that rendezvous was kept in a magnificent way. " Separated by many miles," he writes from Lavagnac to one of his friends, " how good it would be for both of us to visit Our Lord on the same day, to see Him, to adore Him as our common Friend who speaks at the same moment to both of us. . . ." This practical application of a doctrine he had reasoned out in the abstract, is typical of d'Alzon at any moment of his career, nor is there any hint of pious sentimentality about it. At no time in his career, to use the fine expression of Canon Galeran, " did he mistake butterflies for angels, nor the flutterings of sentimental piety for the deep living of a truth." Or to use d'Alzon's own phrase, he was never one "who showed the whites of his eyes" in his devotional practices. When he opened his heart in a letter to a friend and spoke out of its abundance, every word carried its weight and there was no vapour.

What impact did he make on his friends and what impression did he leave? We are fortunate in having quite a wealth of testimony on which to draw. For Dr. Menard, a member of the *Bonnes Etudes*, the memory of d'Alzon was bracketed with that of Lacordaire and Dupanloup, though fifty years had gone by since those meetings *chez Bailly :* " While still too young to have found his way, d'Alzon seemed to bear already the mark of a man chosen for big things. That is why, for me, his memory lives vividly with that of P. Lacordaire and Mgr. Dupanloup." In the letters he wrote to his friends, Emmanuel put into practice those words of his article on friendship : " A friend's words should do for a disturbed heart what the swans do for the lake. Their floating smoothes the waters, and a friend also calms storms, but with this difference : the calm on the waters is as short-lived as the passage of the swan which produces it, while the friend, on the contrary, brings long and abiding peace." His companions in the *Bonnes Etudes* felt his departure keenly, when he left Paris for Lavagnac in 1830 : " Your departure, d'Alzon," wrote Du Lac, " has afflicted us. When your friends met together the other day, we said to one another : d'Alzon is so good for us, with his fresh and virginal soul ; he pours a soothing balm on our troubled hearts when we are in need of comfort."

The phrase *fresh and virginal soul* stands out here in letters of light. The secret of his influence over his friends was that purity of vision, that cleanness of heart which made them turn to him with confidence as their guide, philosopher and friend. " I open my heart to you ", writes one of his friends, " because I am sure you have been put in the way of my earthly pilgrimage to encourage me to love God." He is not afraid to speak roundly to a friend who has betrayed the great promise in him by turning to a silly swirl of social stupidities :

" *Ah, what a grand sight ! . . . A fine young man, gifted in mind and in body, becomes a meaningless eddy, no longer knowing where he is, seeking constant distraction, taking every precaution lest fatigue or boredom should make him say : I have done nothing that an ape or a bear could not have done as well, for an ape or bear can dance and throw contortions. What a trembling in the heart when one has a young girl in one's arms—when to right and left are young girls, young girls on all sides ! Ah, the marvel of these young girls ! To-morrow, faded ; the following day old, with wigs and false teeth ; and then a mass of worms between four boards ! Courage, my good friend, go on ! Dance, laugh, make sure you waste your time ! But be assured of this, that there is one whose eyes will be filled with tears, whose heart will be captive to sadness and chagrin, every time he remembers that his friend—his friend with the big heart, with the foursquare and shining spirit—is wallowing in follies, losing his time and diminishing himself to the mean ambition of being thought ' a fine fellow . . .' Let us both endeavour to learn wisdom, let us look one another full in the eyes. For it seems to me that the eye of a friend has the same virtue as those of certain animals : first, it sees the threatening darkness, and then it freezes to death those little vermin which are eating at our hearts . . ."*

It is easy to read this and to see years hence Father Emmanuel d'Alzon standing before a stubborn sinner and drawing out a blood-stained handkerchief to show what her conversion was costing him. In friendship, in his relations with men, there were no half measures with d'Alzon, nor any of that self-interest which so often hides behind the mask of friendship. " D'Alzon was no self-seeker," wrote one of his friends as early as 1830, " for there was a great disinterestedness in his relations with his friends." When he devoted himself to the good of his friends and gave them wise counsel, he did so without any hint of superiority or desire to dominate. Because they recognized the simplicity, the genuine concern, the purity of d'Alzon, his friends turned to him, and they were met with a warmth that went to the cold places in them when they most needed consolation, but which never flattered. *" The praises which I hear lavished on my friends,"* he writes, *" always give me exquisite pleasure. . . ." " For my part, my friends are older than I am, and therefore more mature in every way and superior to me. . . . Their successes delight me, for it is my nature to make myself so one with my friends that their successes become mine. Perhaps there is a little pride in this—but no matter, for it is a pride which does no harm to anyone !* "

We conclude our impression of d'Alzon the friend with what is perhaps his most lyrical paragraph. It is struck off at white heat, and expresses the warm attitude of the young man of nineteen to that high ideal of friendship he so often voiced. The language is, of course, typical of the 1840's when Romanticism was in the air, but the sentiments have a backbone of sincerity which makes the whole ring true. "*Love then, let us love ! But we need not rush forward to seize the fleeting hour. Time will not steal from you the beauty which I love in you. I have no fear that your soul will shrivel, especially if you sometimes, nay often, bring it close to the principle of all love, I mean to beautiful, holy, generous love, in such a way that your heart will expand to beauty every day.*"

We have deliberately stressed the great importance which d'Alzon attached to friendship, his exalted idea of it, and his genius for it. He himself developed spiritually through his relations with his friends, and it was the great purpose of his friendship with them that they should develop through their relations with him. He was destined to become the founder of a new religious family in the Church—the family of the Assumption. You could almost define a man with the stuff of a religious founder in him, as one who is a genius in friendship as d'Alzon understood friendship. For such a one is capable of gathering men into a unity, a oneness, of friendship which has God for its beating heart. There is a consistency in the life-pattern of Emmanuel d'Alzon, and his greatness is foreshadowed fully in those student years. When his friends wished to express this, they naturally remembered that tribute of Saint Gregory to his friend Saint Basil : " An orator among the orators, even before he seated himself in the chair of eloquence ; a philosopher before the dogmas of philosophy ; and, what is greatest of all, a priest for Christians even before the priesthood " —and applied them to their friend d'Alzon. Indeed, to say that a man has an angelically pure heart and a genius for friendship as the pure heart knows friendship, all being impregnated with the love of God, is to say that such a man will sweep his world like a prairie fire. The orator, the philosopher, the friend, the priest were all taking shape in the student d'Alzon, and his whole life was shaping itself to the height of his next decision which would set his foot firmly towards the altar of God.

Enthusiasm was the key-note to his attitude to friendship, as enthusiasm was the keynote to the whole man. In May, 1830, he left Paris because of the political situation and arrived at Lavagnac six days later. From then until March 14th, 1832, Emmanuel lived at Lavagnac, devoting himself to literary, juridical, philosophical and theological studies according to a very severe plan which he imposed on himself. This plan was generously seasoned with prayer and exercises of piety. On May 16th, 1830, the Chamber of Deputies was dissolved and the elections were fixed for June and July. In due course, his father was elected at Montpellier, but on July 25th Polignac annulled the elections which were unfavourable to him, and the revolution broke out in Paris which removed the elder branch of the Bourbons and called the family of Orléans to the throne. This change of régime caused Vicomte d'Alzon to abandon politics, and also decided Emmanuel to remain with him at Lavagnac. For Emmanuel, it meant two years of intensely individual study ranging from Plato to Don Quixote, but with nothing of dilettantism about it. The dilettante browses here and there according to whim and with no fixed direction or aim. D'Alzon's varied study of philosophy, sacred and profane history, poetry, eloquence, Sacred Scripture, Theology, was all directed by and towards that master aim which he had formulated at the end of 1828 : " I wish to consecrate myself entirely to the defence of the Church and of religion." At his request, Lamennais had drawn up a programme of study and a daily agenda for him. D'Alzon kept strictly to it and even increased its severity. He rose at six; prayed and meditated till seven; studied Holy Scripture till eight; assisted at Mass; breakfast and the chase followed; he worked from eleven to five, and again for two hours before retiring to sleep at eleven o'clock. In 1830, the higher studies were absolutely in ruins, overwhelmed by the terrible blow of the great Revolution and by the wars of the Empire. Politics filled all France, and especially the Midi, with its disturbances. For the moment, Emmanuel turned from it all, and, in his own phrase, "dug himself into his books". Those two years of intense work were to be of immense value to him all his life, for they meant that, intellectually, he had begun his career with a purposeful leap ahead.

And yet—no mere bookworm, but a man whose real book was human life where he learned with his heart. "Without looking beyond the short period from 1828 to 1832," writes Father Picard, "we find in this predestined young man a student of immense intellectual energy, an incomparable friend, the virtue of a saint, the zeal of an apostle."

The zeal of an apostle : we have seen evidence of this in his concern for the spiritual welfare of his friends, but it took another form which Emmanuel kept a close secret, revealing it only to his mother, and later—because circumstances compelled him—to one of his aunts. While a student in Paris, he used to make his way several times a week to the *quartier Notre Dame* where stood that famous Hôtel-Dieu which Vincent de Paul knew so well. How that same Vincent must have rejoiced to see this aristocrat of his country, this son of a proud Christian lineage, walking the wards of that crowded hospital to bring a ray of consolation and of hope to so many poor wretches. "*All the patients to whom I have spoken," he writes, " have shown themselves well disposed. Here is my usual method : when I come to them for the first time, I chat with them only about their health, their profession, and so on, and end by urging them gently to bear their hard lot with patience ; it is only on the second visit that I speak a little seriously to them and that I touch on religious duties. I do not wish you (his mother) to speak to anyone about this.*" This was an aspect of his student days that none of his friends knew of, and it showed him the stark reality of human suffering that he might learn to plumb its depths. "To spiritual alms," writes Father Picard, "Emmanuel joined temporal. In this connection, we see him showing the innate generosity of his nature. His mother used to give him regularly a certain sum of money, and he was always without a sou! He used to give away everything. He would give to works of propaganda ; to the poor, whom he never refused ; to his friends when they were in need ; to his patients in the Hôtel-Dieu. This reached such a pitch that, at this period, Madame d'Alzon was obliged to pull tight the strings of her purse, for Emmanuel had already the bad habit of drawing on *his month* two or three times in advance. Nevertheless, his expenses came under only two heads : his library and his good works. . . ." Poor Madame d'Alzon ! She was always to have that same financial trouble with her son, the fingers of whose hand were so spread out by charity that money went easily through them. The pattern of his charity would remain always the same—there would be no nice " prudence ", no " neatness " about his charity, and Madame would have many moments of annoyance and, one suspects, of a secret joy which she would not admit even to herself.

To complete this picture of d'Alzon, the student-apostle, we must turn to those two years of studious retirement at Lavagnac, where we are amazed to discover that he found time in such a full programme for works of charity. In Paris, he had come face to face with suffering ; at Lavagnac, among the peasants of the estate, he came face to face for the first time with hunger. There was one story which he heard discussed shortly after his return to Lavagnac, and which sent a thrill of horror through him. It concerned a certain gravedigger who was so poor that he had but one bed for himself, his wife and his five children. That sounds like the opening sentence of a fairy story, but the fact is all too clearly recorded by Father Picard. The only joy that entered that house was the joy of hearing the death-knell tolling its good tidings that there was a new grave to be opened ! It was a terrible thought that people should have to depend on a corpse for their crust of bread. Disturbed and thoughtful after having heard this tale, d'Alzon went up to his room and wrote this comment : " *The six years I have spent in Paris have given me no idea of anything so sad as one month of winter here. This one month has shown me HUNGER !* " It was a new challenge to him, and he turned to meet it.

About this time, his best friend wrote to him to say he was about to get married. D'Alzon too could get married : the admiring murmurs of ' What a distinguished young man ' which came to him in the *salons*, showed that he could have chosen from many. He chose instead to marry the misery, the ignorance, the strivings of his fellow men, as he said magnificently in his reply:

"*May you be happy in the bosom of the family which God will cause to be born to you. For my part, I feel my heart is made for another paternity. Yes, that is indeed so. My heart opens wide that I may love with a universal love ; I form for myself an idea of the immensity which is the heart of a priest, and I think I am beginning to have just such a heart within me. Ah, my dear friend, you do not know what it is, like Saint Paul, to be in labour with Christians until Jesus Christ is formed in them. In my instructions to the servants of our house, I myself serve a very sweet apprenticeship. Of four or five families, I make but one family of which I am the bond, and I unite that one family to Christ. My friend, if you do not understand this kind of happiness, sympathize with yourself, for you are blind to great joys !*"

The *apprenticeship* he refers to is the apprenticeship to compassion, to love, to the joy of selfless love. He served these good people, he instructed them, he did all in his power to sweeten life's burden for them. In doing so, he tasted joy as only one of his purity could taste it.

We have seen the many-splendoured character of the student Emmanuel d'Alzon. All the energy and power of his ancestral line have come alive, and are controlled and directed by a burning enthusiasm, a passion for purity, a thirst for union with Christ. "*It has come at last, it has come,*" he writes excitedly ; "*that ENTHUSIASM which has always been growing in me every time I approach the Holy Table of Communion. It has taken possession of me. . . .*" This enthusiasm was not some incidental malady of late adolescence ; it was something lasting because it was, and always would be fed on prayer. "*By prayer,*" he writes in 1830, "*the soul acquires a new faculty which brings into its ken an order of things of which it could alone form no conception. I feel that prayer sometimes carries me to the very threshold of this order of things, that the door sometimes stands ajar so that I may glimpse what I might enjoy, were I sufficiently pure to enter. . . .*" This is the voice of that authentic " hunger and thirst after justice " which made him write : "*I aim to be a saint.*" There was no pride in this, for there was no pride in d'Alzon. Pride is the vice of the small man, of " the narrow spirit " ; his was a big spirit, for he was

in every sense a big man.   For all his famous independence of
spirit, and we shall have occasion to see many examples of it,
his spirit was always on its knees in the dust of its own nothingness.   Even as a student, he was already among those who, in
Mgr. Besson's fine phrase, know " the secret of continuing to
stand even when they kneel."   Christian humility and Christian
pride were the colours of the sanctity of Emmanuel d'Alzon,
and purity was the great, throbbing source of it all.   From this
was born that enthusiasm which set his years ablaze.

Tête de roi, coeur de séraphin, they were to say of him in the
streets of Nîmes.   *Regal head, seraphic heart*—and that immensity
which is the heart of a great priest.

THE SHAPING OF A LIFE'S IDEAL

WE HAVE a passage in one of Emmanuel d'Alzon's letters in which he traces the growth of his religious vocation, in answer to a friend who considered it as a passing fancy : " From the age of ten to the age of twelve, the idea of becoming a priest was my great pleasure. I abandoned it for some time, and the career which seemed most attractive was that of the army. This, however, I set aside, persuaded to do so by my parents. But, from about that time, *I decided to devote myself to the defence of religion* and this idea took shape within me in an amazing way. I admit that henceforward I felt a keen repugnance for public functions. . . ." The vocation of Emmanuel d'Alzon for the priesthood was an *intellectual* one ; it was the vocation of a young man who wished to enter the lists of intellectual and spiritual combat, but who saw no cause worthy of him except that growing and God-given desire of his to devote himself to the defence of religion. It needed only a sharpening of outline to convert this resolve into a definite call to the priesthood. It required, however, great purity of vision to effect this resolve, for it was taken in spite of strong, persuasive opposition. Though he had decided on what course he was to take as early as 1829, he had to conquer three years of strong and well-intentioned dissuasion, as well as moments of internal struggle. Only a truly supernatural vocation could have stood up to them.

It is against the opinion generally held of the priesthood in post-Revolutionary France that we first see that vocation pitted. The clerical life was at a low ebb in public esteem. Except for rare exceptions of which the ill-starred Abbé Lamennais was the most conspicuous example, the clergy had not yet had the means of regaining the standard and the level they had held before the great Revolution. The upper classes now scarcely ever furnished recruits for the sanctuary. The middle classes—university-trained, sceptical, Voltairean—dis-

trusted the clerical cassock and mocked at it.   Even among the
cream of the people, the group that centred around M. Bailly
in the *Société Littéraire*, there was something of this prejudice,
as witness their bewilderment and amazement when Lacordaire
disappeared into the Seminary at Issy.   There was a strange
conviction among these intellectuals, that a man would lay
aside half his power of doing good were he to take to wearing
a cassock.   We shall see how his friends put this forward when
d'Alzon announced his decision.   Yet, these were part of a
little oasis of live Catholicism, grouped about a few eminent men,
and around them was a desert of torpor and indifference.   Some
of the dust of that desert, the pervasive prejudice settling
everywhere, showed itself even in the oasis.   It is easy to choose
the priesthood in a country like Ireland where it is held in awe,
and indeed such awe can give danger to the choice ; but in the
France of the nineteenth century, it argued the single eye and the
purity of intention required for a good priest, in the man—above
all in the aristocrat—who chose the priesthood.   It is in such
a twilight of prejudice that we must hear those enthusiastic
words of d'Alzon : " *How admirable is the position of the priest
to-day !* "

It seems clear that the date on which he finally and irrevocably
made his decision was August 19th, 1829, the Feast of Saint
Bernard.   This day was to be always sacred to him, and the
decision which it marked was the end of a month of terrible
interior resistance to his vocation.   " *What a wretch I am !* "
he wrote later.   " *For a whole month I have resisted my vocation,
but my conversion has come on the Feast of Saint Bernard.   I have
conquered my temptation.* "   The saint's feast had a certain significance.   Like Saint Bernard, d'Alzon was to find himself engaged
in all the affairs of the Church, without having any official rôle
and with no desire of honour or of dignity.   He flung the circle
of his zeal with enthusiasm, and it was a splendid circle, while
he himself was content, in his own words, " to be a simple
worker for the regeneration of the world."

He spoke of his " *personal vocation* " in words which show
what a consuming fire was to meet the straws of objection thrown
in the way of that vocation.   He spoke as a man who is gripped

by, intoxicated by, that vocation. "*Oh, if I could ever realize the model which has been shown to me !*" he writes. "*If I could but incarnate the idea I have of my personal vocation ! If I could accomplish my mission to men, and at the same time become as one crucified to the world—place my hands on the Hands of Christ, my feet on His Feet, my heart in His Heart, and suffer with Him.* The sufferings of a priest are very beautiful, when they are considered, not as expiation, not as personal cross, but AS SACRIFICE FOR OTHERS. . . . This is real happiness !*"* . . . His ideal of the priesthood is, therefore, the lofty one of a priest crucified in heart with the crucified Christ, and offering himself for *others*. "*The life of the priest,*" he wrote, "*is the life of the Cross. . . . The privilege of the priest is to learn, through sorrow, the mysteries of mercy.*" "*Here is true happiness !*" he again wrote. "*I shall be a priest, and, like Jesus Christ, a priest for others !*" In such a pure and lofty way did the priesthood present itself to one who had not yet taken the first step. His pure soul reached out to it, and it was in vain that voices were raised against his choice.

His friends seemed unanimously against him. "You will have a thousand times more influence for good if you avoid the cassock," wrote one of them. Another painted a harrowing picture of the priest who regrets his choice too late. A priest has told d'Alzon that he was born for the priesthood—but take care, Emmanuel, the friendly voice insists, that this priest is not concerned to fill, in *any* way, the gaps in the ranks of the Clergy ! With his eyes raised to the ideal of the priesthood he had formed for himself, d'Alzon was entirely uninfluenced by those appeals to fulfil his destiny as a great layman, 'the apostle of the *salon*', the Christian father of a Christian family. These suggestions were splendid ones ; the trouble was that they were not splendid enough. "*If I explained to you,*" he replied, "*how I look on the character of the priest, you would no longer find it inaccessbile to friendship, nor would you think of the cassock as a garment of brass. . . .*" The cassock would be for d'Alzon the outward sign that its wearer had learned, through suffering, the mysteries of mercy.

"*Now,*" he writes on November 7th, 1831, referring to his decision to tell his parents, "*the time has come to break the silence I have kept, and to break it with joy, for I have no sadness in me. . . .*"

He had held back from telling his parents, for he knew what hopes they had built on him. He had everything—fortune, a magnificent château, a youth of brilliance, success, popularity, all pointing to a magnificent career in the world; and the glory of the d'Alzon line was in his hands to pass on. Again, it was particularly true of the *Midi* that the clergy were recruited almost exclusively from the lower classes. However Christian they were, his family and the people of his district could scarcely believe that a gentleman of the young d'Alzon's rank would shut himself in a Seminary, for the idea of a Seminary was certainly not a flattering one in the 1830's, and the current of prejudice made recruiting for the Church a very difficult matter indeed. The surprise with which his parents received the news can therefore be imagined; and, taking all these things into consideration, their Christian attitude was deserving of the highest praise. "We shall place no obstacle in your way," his mother assured him, "but we wish you to conisder the matter for a year. You will live with us and among your relations; no one will attempt to influence you; you yourself will not even speak of your intentions; and, at the end of that year, during which God alone will speak with you, if He still calls you, you will go." Poor Madame d'Alzon! She certainly would not oppose the will of God, but who can guess the hopes with which she filled those months of silence in which no amount of taboo could remove the great question-mark she saw always? Years before, that son of hers had written: "*For some time now, I have been discovering in myself as it were a new man. . . .*" Madame d'Alzon had borne a man; but grace had given birth to another man within that man, *a new man* in the Pauline sense of the word, and it was with that new man that she was now dealing. Those months, too, were a time of trial for Emmanuel. After having "broken silence with joy" to his parents, he seems to have again passed through a short period of depression, which he himself described by the image of flame and smoke. "*It is true, indeed,*" he writes, "*that a little constancy causes the smoke to pass and the light to shine out again. . . . The smoke has passed or is disappearing little by little, and every day I see the flame more and more, or rather I feel it. What a powerful source of happiness it is !* " This flame stood up straight in his life, beckoning him ; and though the matter was never discussed, it was clear, as month followed month, that his resolve had the strength of a real vocation. His parents submitted to the will of God, and made one small concession to themselves and their sorrow. It was tacitly agreed that Emmanuel should leave for the Seminary of Montpellier secretly, so that the painful separation would take place under a kind of anæsthetic.

Father Picard has described that final parting. " On March 14th, 1832, after having dined as usual with the family, he went to the drawing-room to have his last conversation with them. He repressed the emotions surging up in him : ' *I held my peace,*' he said later, ' *but though I was master of myself, my heart was in unbelievable turmoil.*' He was anxiously watching the clock, for he must give the domestics time to have their meal. At a calculated moment, he slipped quietly from the conversation, from the adieus, from the very legitimate outbursts of affection. . . . This silent separation caused him acute suffering, of which he was to say later to his friends : ' *Most certainly you have not experienced a separation like that which I have had to endure.*' He descended quietly from his room to a court which was remote from the drawing-room in which he had passed the evening. The carriage awaited him there, and he asked that no attention should be drawn to his departure." He was making a connection with the public coach which was to bring him through the night to Montpellier, where he would present himself at the Seminary in the morning. We owe a last detail to a Doctor Privat who happened to be travelling by the same coach. The last appeal to d'Alzon to turn back, came from the servant who accompanied him. This good man had his memories of the many kindnesses which attached him to the young master. He stood in tears, affectionately angry with the young master, refusing to lift his bags on to the public coach, pleading the sorrow of Madame his mother, and opening again all the emotional wounds of Emmanuel so that his heart bled again. Emmanuel pulled himself energetically together, told the servant to be quiet, seized the bags and leaped on to the coach.

Back in the drawing-room at Lavagnac, quarter-hour followed

quarter-hour, and he did not come back. Both his mother and his father knew that they might expect his departure from one day to the next. And now, in the silence of that room, they knew it had come. "My uncle and aunt," writes that cousin who was to become Sister Charlotte, "retired to their room without speaking a word. Augustine and Marie, his sisters, did the same, in order to give free vent to their tears. A general atmosphere of mourning took the whole household. . . . Two days later, my aunt came to Montpellier with her two daughters. I ran to meet her. She embraced me, and her tears were wet on my cheeks. She said to me: 'My child, you know the full measure of sacrifice which the good God asks of me; but if it were necessary for me merely to walk to yonder crossing or to take two steps in my room, in order to make Emmanuel leave the Seminary, I would not do it. *I would fear that I was going against the will of God.*'" Here indeed is the strong voice of faith speaking clearly and with conviction, in spite of the strangling grip of human emotions: the woman of faith conquering the woman of flesh and blood. It was moments like these that made Emmanuel d'Alzon proud of his mother, and showed him just how much he owed to his inheritance from her.

D'Alzon's entry into the Seminary of Montpellier was something of a sensation. For a few days, the students saw that tall, aristocratic figure moving about their cloisters, clothed in a rich mantle with a collar and lining of red velvet, such as was in use among the aristocracy. Then, shortly after his arrival, they saw him emerge from his cell, dressed in a plain cassock. But they did not forget that flash of red velvet, and from the very outset he had to bear the cross of their not accepting him, even while their own manners and manner of acting must have jarred on him. He could not lay aside his upbringing as he had laid aside that red velvet, and it was inevitable that some of his companions should read into his conduct a tacit criticism of their own. We do not imply that their conduct and bearing were unworthy of their calling; it sufficed that they were *different*, so that d'Alzon stood out from them as singular to the point of being unique. Had they but known it, however, this aristocrat was in the dust at their feet, as witness this extract from one of his letters : " *Why am I in the Seminary?* " he quotes from a letter of protest. " *I assure you, who are my friend, that I do not even dare to say that I love God, when I see so many young men, on whom Providence has lavished gifts so less abundantly, making such efforts to respond to the graces given them at the very time when I languish in inexcusable torpor. Oh, my confusion is great!* "

His professors misunderstood him, too, and they certainly must be excused for that! The Seminaries exist for the training of priests for the parochial ministry, and, even though their curriculum and methods at that time left something to be desired, they were not nearly as bad as intellectuals like Lamennais, Montalembert and d'Alzon seemed to have considered them. D'Alzon indeed took up the cudgels in defence of the Seminary against the critics : " *I do not understand how anyone can be a critic of the seminary who was never a seminarian. Is there really a ' narrowness' in it? Is hiding oneself in God a synonym for going mouldy? Is the charm of an ordered life to be called monotony? . . .*" These were his answers to men like Montalembert who wrote to him of " that *moral and intellectual oppression* which is called the life of the seminary " ; of " narrowness " in which the mind must get narrow, of that strange thing that one of them called " the odour of the seminary." D'Alzon was critical of the seminary, but his criticism began beyond all such pettiness. The clear fact of the matter seems to have been that he was a square peg in a round hole, a man never designed for the parochial ministry placed in the mould of such ministry. " All the seminaries of France put together," Lamennais wrote to him, " are absolutely null as far as instruction is concerned." D'Alzon would not have endorsed that, but he was prepared to go half-way. " *I would not set myself up as the champion of the method of present-day seminarist studies,*" he writes. " *I know that they have great faults which will paralyse for a long time to come the action of the Clergy. In our theological conferences, the students hold useless disputations, making theological pettifoggers of themselves and missing the spirit of the doctrine. Time is lost in hairsplitting about bagatelles, while essential questions are left untouched. . . .*" A man as honest as d'Alzon would show this attitude of his in some way or other, however careful he was. It is not surprising, therefore, that his professors should have misunderstood him for a while. It can be quite irritating when you are fitting round pegs into round holes and you suddenly come on a square one. D'Alzon was a square peg, because both his mental background and his energy of outlook made him far too big for the mould. Yet, it would give a completely one-sided view of him, were we to omit his tribute to the worth of that very mould : " *I return to the seminary* ", he writes, " *with mixed feelings of sorrow and of joy. Of joy, because community life is necessary for me in the greatest measure. You have no idea how advantageously one's time is employed by living according to rule. Even the mind gains by it. I am beginning to lose my taste for that vagueness which goes with a completely free life in which much time is lost for self and for God. . . .*" Like Wordsworth on the merits of the sonnet's laws, he finds it "pleasure to be bound " to rule because he fears " the weight of too much liberty." He was not satisfied, however, with the amount of instruction or with the speed of progress. The solution which could combine the discipline with the intellectual liberty he required, was to come later, when, as a student in Rome, he kept to his cell and became a " freelance " student at the feet of chosen and diverse masters. Meantime, his period at Montpellier was one of tension and of trial for him.

His position there was not improved by his known relations with Lamennais. Whispers, hypotheses, suspicions grew up around him in the seminary, fanned by that gossiping that tittle-tattle, which he hated so much. " *There are absurd rumours about me and my projects circulating in the seminary* ", he writes. Lamennais had come under suspicion, and the great leader of a new renaissance was rapidly on his way to becoming a noted heresiarch. All this added to the discomfort of his position. " *What I have said, my dear father,*" he writes, " *must remain strictly between ourselves, because, sooner or later, some indiscretion may have the effect of putting me in a position of acute embarrassment with my superiors. . . .*" Words like these throw great light on his state of mind in Montpellier. And yet, in spite of it all, his spiritual progress there was remarkable. During his holidays at Lavagnac, he applied himself to acquire what he called " *master-ideas—that is to say, principles calculated to make fertile the minds of those who are called, by their vocation, to assume some leadership over men ; ideas whose absence from the mental armoury of certain priests leaves those priests without influence over society.*" The master-idea among all such master-ideas for him was, of course, the priesthood, and it grew within him during that Montpellier period as the great central source of unity and of meaning. At a time when Lamennais was developing rapidly towards his doctrine of the Church's social bankruptcy, his pupil d'Alzon was showing in no uncertain manner just how far he was prepared to accompany him along that road :

"*My friend,*" he writes, "*it is becoming more and more clear to me that there is still sufficient power, still sufficient vital energy in Catholicism to renew the face of France and of Europe through love. But who will be able to bring this love among men? Oh, how beautiful will be his mission if, taking a live coal from the altar, as the Seraphim did in Isaias' vision, he purifies the lips of men !* "

There is a buoyant optimism here which refuses to see the present and the future as a dark mass of hopeless shadow. He knew, as he said to his sister Augustine, that God was " choosing those who had been most faithful to Him " in order to send them forth " to re-Catholicize Europe." Again, in a letter to his friend d'Esgrigny, he wrote : " *I watch intently that great battle of the good and evil, in which I am called to take an active part. . . . The fruit of all those reflections which constantly fill my mind, is a violent desire to contribute, with all my strength and to the limits of my powers, to the great regeneration which is coming. . . .*" It is easy to see that a soul obsessed with such apostolic dreams must have found the limits and the vision of Montpellier somewhat cramping. We are not surprised, therefore, to find d'Alzon, at the age of twenty-three, writing to Lamennais that he was not returning to Montpellier because he did not find there the science he knew he must acquire. The Lamennais group, among whom were the inestimable Abbés Gerbet and de Salinis, were immediately insistent that he should join them in Paris and continue his studies for the priesthood there. This appealed greatly to him ; but once again, in deference to his parents who were acutely alive to the dangerous tendencies of *L'Avenir*, he set his own wishes aside. This humble filial deference was rewarded a hundredfold. He chose Rome. In the designs of God, this early contact with Rome was to be a very vital factor in the shaping of a man whose life's absorbing passion was devotion to the Church, and who was chosen by God to found a Congregation on which he would stamp that devotion as its great characteristic. His Roman period was to bring him into the storm centring around the name of Lamennais, and he was to emerge from it with a deeply learnt lesson. " *For me* ", he had once written to d'Esgrigny, " *the way is a stony one, shadowed, and filled with thorns.*" That period in Rome was to be such for d'Alzon, for it was shadowed by his anxiety for the welfare of Lamennais, the man whom he loved, the priest who had helped his ideal of the priesthood, and who was now hurtling to spiritual destruction down the slope of his own pride.

When, on April 11th, 1828, Emmanuel d'Alzon met the Abbé Féli de Lamennais for the first time, he must have felt his heart go out to him as to a kindred soul of energy and of fire. A man of 46 in 1828, Lamennais had brought his great talents to the challenge of a France in which the Church was " in a struggling and precarious condition, deprived of material resources and served but poorly by a clergy either enfeebled by age or inadequately prepared to meet the intellectual demands of the time." We are concerned here with his story only as it affected d'Alzon, for it is the sad story of a man whose vigorous campaign against Gallicanism and moribund Catholicism lifted him to a height of popularity to which his humility was unequal when the time for humble submission came. At the now historical la Chênaie, he had established an intellectual nucleus which bid fair to be the renaissance of religion in France ; as early as 1817, the year of his ordination to the priesthood, had come his magnificent *Essai sur l'indifference* which lifted Catholic apologetics out of the doldrums and gave it a new strength and brilliance. France suddenly woke up to this new voice that came with a sharp, definite crispness into the chatter of the ignorant and the half-educated ; the brilliance of it all reached the Vatican, and the Pope in joy saluted " the light of the latest Father of the Church."

One's virtue needs an excellent head for emotional heights when the cymbals of praise clash and the laudatory orchids are handed out with enthusiastic abandon. Lamennais had no head for it all. He began with the brilliant apologetics of the *Essai*, an intellectual sword lifted challengingly. It was the glint of that sword that called to the soldier in d'Alzon who looked to Lamennais as " the master." The organ of Lamennais and his party was the newspaper *L'Avenir*, which went from one boldness to another until it came under ecclesiastical censure. There followed the famous pilgrimage of " the three pilgrims of God and of Liberty "—Lamennais, Lacordaire and Montalembert— to plead their cause at Rome. They spent some months of 1831 and 1832 in Rome, but without obtaining any definite decision. They were on what was virtually a triumphant tour, and were being fêted at Munich when the Encyclical *Mirari Vos* reached them. *L'Avenir* was not expressly named, but the doctrines it advocated—revolt against princes, liberty of conscience, the need for regenerating Catholicism, etc.—were condemned. There were always two men side by side in the character of Lamennais : the priest and the demagogue. Now the priest faded and the demagogue took over completely. He made a show of submission and went into a kind of sullen, growling retirement at La Chênaie. When asked to give formal adherence to the Encyclical, he quibbled and qualified. Finally, came that day when he sent urgently for Sainte-Beuve and gave him a small manuscript called *Paroles d'un Croyant* for immediate publication. The *Paroles* was an apocalyptic patchwork of prayers and of blasphemies—a bitter book, child of an embittered mind. The Encyclical *Singulari nos*, July 15th, 1834, condemned this book " small in size but great in evil." The demagogue Lamennais had won through, and the rupture with the Church was complete.

All this did not happen, of course, with the calmness of words on paper ; human feelings entered into it, and a man of Lamennais' stature could certainly count on a rush to arms in his defence. Prior to the publication of *Paroles d' un Croyant*, sides were taken in Rome on " the Lamennais affair ". In the opposition camp were Father Rozaven and the Jesuits, whose cause was seconded by the ambassadors and strengthened by political influences; while the colonels in the Lamennais camp were Father Ventura a Theatine and the Pope's theologian, and Father Olivieri soon to become Father General of the Dominican Order, who were supported by many eminent theologians in their belief that Lamennais was in good faith and the victim of persecution. Besides their faith in Lamennais, these men were firmly and rightly convinced that the powerful enemies of the Church and of the Holy See were gleefully awaiting the downfall of one whose book *Essai sur l'indifference*—" capable of rousing a corpse to action ", the critics had said of it—had run like fire through the cold veins of religious indifference and had shaken Europe out of its torpor. Prussia, Austria and Russia had joined with the government of France in denouncing the incendiary writings of this man who had become the fanatical zealot of liberty and of a *universal republic* of which kings and priests were the enemies. "Monseigneur," the Russian ambassador is reported to have said, " the Abbé de Lamennais wishes to turn Catholicism into a colossus, and we will not allow that ! " This was indeed true ; but the Lamennais group in Rome were in the dark as to what was really happening, and many of them had the disadvantage of having to judge the matter through a haze of personal devotion and friendship for Lamennais himself. As their guest in Rome in 1831 and 1832, his personality and verve had cast a spell on them—a spell that was soon to be broken in varied expressions of disillusionment. Thus we shall find Gerbet, one of the early group at La Chênaie and a fervent defender of Lamennais, expressing himself with typical vividness : " The man has undermined the walls of the temple, and at the moment when he sees the pillars swaying and the roof caving in, he attempts, through sentimental veneration, to save the sanctuary lamp and set it up in the market place where the winds will soon quench its flame. . . ." This is indeed a striking metaphor of what Lamennais had fondly tried to do.

All this was at its height when d'Alzon came to Rome as a student in November, 1833. His friends were all in the Lamennais camp ; they were older than he, experienced theologians, men of great intellectual and spiritual substance, while he was a student of twenty-three. It would have been natural, therefore, considering his whole-hearted admiration for Lamennais, if he had become quite ardently pro-Lamennais. It is a splendid tribute to his essential balance of judgment that he did not do so. To adopt a phrase of his own, he diluted the wine of his personal enthusiasm with the water of prudence. He had need to do so, for his position was a very delicate one. No sooner had he come to Rome than Lamennais made him the channel of communication, through his letters to him, with the Lamennais camp in Rome.

"Imagine", writes Father Picard, "the situation of this young man, alone in a Rome furrowed by these great questions ; alone before theologians renowned for sanctity and learning, with the noise of contradictory opinions loud about him ; obliged to serve as intermediary to a master whom he loved but who was in the dock—a master, moreover, whose uncertain attitude and disingenuous letters occasioned him the utmost embarrassment. . . ." This was the crucible time for Emmanuel d'Alzon. Of all those in the Lamennais story, he was perhaps nearest to "the master" in fiery temperament and character. Without that humility and stiff reining of self which he had laboriously cultivated, and the absence of which caused the worm of pride to play havoc with the spiritual structure of Lamennais—for one must dig deep to build high—d'Alzon's story would have ended tragically in the apostate shadow of his master. Indeed, we get some idea of what was lost to the Church by the pride of Lamennais, when we see what was gained for the years to come by the humility and restraint of d'Alzon.

He did not rush in : he waited, he watched, he weighed up everything. He had too sharp an intellect ever to become a myopic and blinkered hero-worshipper. "*I take this and I leave that*", sums up his attitude in his conversations with the theological eminences on both sides. He is, of course, anxious that Lamennais should be cleared, but he is very critical of the pro-Lamennais group whose attitude he gets with a fine simile. "*The Jesuits*", he writes, "*may be wrong in spite of their personal holiness ; but when I see those of the other camp, I tremble at their rashness. They seem to me like postillions who, meeting a steep hill and fearing lest the weight of the coach should tumble the horses, whip the horses into a wild gallop at the risk of breaking their necks. In the final amalysis, I am convinced that, if they are prudent, victory will be on their side ; that is, of course, unless it pleases God to push one camp to the right and the other to the left of Him, to take care of the whole business Himself in order to show that He is the Master.''* There was no danger that d'Alzon would mount that coach and join in the whipping. As his simile shows, he suspected that his friends were too eager to push their cause, and he saw in that eagerness, if we consider the simile closely, a suspicion that perhaps they were whipping themselves and their cause into a frenzy in order to avoid facing about and meeting the real issues. When at last they were forced to rein those foam-flecked horses of theirs, they looked behind to meet the grey sky of their own disillusionment, and some of them uttered bitter words. It is amazing how d'Alzon took the pulse of the whole situation very shortly after he arrived in Rome ; and how he looked at the men and took their measure. "Alone before theologians renowned for sanctity and learning . . ." we have quoted from Picard. Listen, for example, to his comment on Ventura : "*I find that he is a man of immense talent, of great clarity, with great powers of logic, great powers of memory, and a fine fund of exaggeration.*" These, be it noted, are the words of a *humble* man, for humility never means either servility or the swathing of one's mind in wool. It was necessary to keep a sharp look-out for just such exaggerations, for Rome was bubbling with rumours. "*You could have no idea*", he writes to his father, "*of the way certain people are spinning rumours here to their heart's content.*" Rumour met him with the news that Combalot was condemned, which he knew was rubbish. Rumour caught up with him again on the street to tell him that Ventura had been exiled to Modena. Strange . . . when at that very moment he was walking away from a conversation with Ventura. . . . And so it went on. Rumour had its message for d'Alzon, that he must redouble his caution !

Meantime, as intermediary to Lamennais, his position was getting more and more delicate, because his master was showing the cloven hoof more and more beneath the robe of submission.

In his letters to Lamennais, he passes on the opinions and situation-analyses of Micara, of Olivieri, of Ventura ; but when he comes to his own comment, it is neither opinion nor analysis but a veritable *cri du coeur*. " *For my own part, Monsieur l'Abbé, if I add my own humble words to those of the great ones, it is because I would have you know the anguish I am suffering because of all this.*" The italics are his own. D'Alzon was a reticent man where his own suffering was concerned, and such words as these are therefore indicative of how much he was tortured by it all. Lamennais had shown himself a friend ; he had taken great trouble to direct him in that period of study at Lavagnac, and d'Alzon was no fair-weather friend. He was faithful to Lamennais when Lamennais was faithful to Truth. When d'Alzon later wrote his final judgment on his master : " *Without Catholicism, Lamennais is nothing* "—the words were not pharisaically cold, for they were written in deep personal pain. The choice between Plato and Truth can be a heartrending one ; the mind sees and accepts, while the heart mourns.

Lamennais' letters began to get heavy with dirge for a dead Catholicism, and apocalyptic prophecy of some shapeless substitute to come—the sanctuary lamp lifted in the vacant breezes of the market-place, as Gerbet had suggested. How it must have rent d'Alzon's heart to hear his master shaping the fine phrase in the service of apostasy and of a strange, proud, apocalyptic despair : " No one is any longer concerned with Catholicism and the Church. They no longer incite either hatred or love. They are regarded as dead—indeed, there is no more general and deep conviction in France than that they are so. In fact, were they to reappear on the political scene, they would be kicked back into their grave." Christianity, he goes on, will undergo a transformation, and the Church a development. What will this development be ? he asks. And he answers : " No one knows ; but all are agreed that it will be incompatible with the present Catholic institution which contains, it is said, a clear and radical antinomy whose solution can be furnished only by a new institution. . . ." The drift of all this was only too clear. These " dominant ideas " were simply the pretension of christianizing Christianity without the christianizer being

Christ; by something better, shaped to the needs of a 'new' humanity, and founded—according to its author's criterion of truth as the *sensus communis*—on a kind of universal suffrage or plebiscite. "The people are ranked above the Church", comments Father Picard, "opinion above faith, man above Christ. God is God and demagogy is his prophet."

With a heavy heart, d'Alzon carried these letters to his friends. We have a record of one scene which serves as typical of many others. D'Alzon had come to Father Ventura and handed him a letter from Lamennais. Ventura began to read: "I think it is no longer possible to defend the Church. I owe a debt of gratitude to my adversaries, whose stupid and sottish hatred has at last shown me that we must leave everything to Providence. . . ." He read no further. The letter dropped from his hand, and he said with a sigh: "I had no idea he had gone so far." Lamennais had written to d'Alzon: "The world is clearly marching to new destinies; the old envelope is tearing in all parts, though the form of the chrysalis is not yet apparent." The words had an ironical application to " the master " himself. He had written his real thoughts in an envelope of fine phrases; but the seams had rent and the chrysalis was only too apparent. His letters dropped out of many hands, and his cause from many hearts.

We owe to Monsieur Bailly, who has already figured in our story, a last sad glimpse of Lamennais. "One day," he writes, "I chanced on the Abbé de Lamennais in a Paris street. I had not seen him for a long time. His miserable lay dress, his appearance, everything about him, spoke his ruin. The passage of time had soothed his bitterness. I felt a sudden urge, I don't know why or how, to ask him a personal question which must have struck home. 'Tell me sincerely and between ourselves, when exactly did you cease to believe in the Real Presence?' He was so taken aback with the forthrightness of my question that he answered sincerely and in a voice heavy with sorrow: 'My dear friend, on the very day after I decided in my heart to resist the authority of the Sovereign Pontiff, I found, when I went to the altar, that I could no longer believe. As you can see, that was the end.' . . ." It was a cold, sad end to a career that had begun so well. Where pride is sown, the crop is darkness and loss of faith. " I saw Satan falling . . ." are Christ's admonitory words when pride began to lift its head among His followers.

This is not the place to linger over the many facets of the relations between Lamennais and d'Alzon; and over the details of the ' Lamennais affair '. There is matter for half a volume in these few years of d'Alzon's life. We are concerned only to notice its significance in the whole pattern of his story. The fate of Lamennais was as a great, living warning on the threshold of life for d'Alzon. " There but for the grace of God go I " was an adage that had a striking relevance here. There were many things in Lamennais which mirrored the character of d'Alzon ; burning energy, tremendous industry, a mind like a rapier, vision and emanating power, chivalry and impetuous devotion to a cause. But the grace of God was there too— that grace which whispered to d'Alzon years before, that the secret of Christian strength is humility, and that the heart of Christian prudence is Christian submission. There is ample evidence that never for one moment did he allow his devotion to Lamennais to alter in any way his attitude of submission to the authority of Rome. In a letter to one of his professors, we have his own statement of what it all cost him, and of what he gained from it all :

" *You wish to know what all these events have meant for me personally. They have caused me great distress, but they have purified my faith, so that it now rests more and more in God and I desire only the good of His Church. Oh, how small, feeble, illusory, is everything apart from this ! Pray God, I beseech you, that I may derive from all that is happening under my very eyes, lessons of humility and of hope. It is sometimes very difficult to keep a firm, two-handed grip on one's soul, and sometimes one is defeated. However, when calm comes again, one is weaker, more broken, more supple, more docile under the hand of God ; and this is as it should be.*

The whole spiritual history of d'Alzon during those crucial years is in that paragraph. He loved and respected the man from whom he was forced to turn away, for he was so like him that, had things turned out otherwise, d'Alzon and Lamennais might have fused into one glowing power as flame loses itself in flame. As it was, however, he drew great strength from the outcome :

"*Every day I watch the course of events, and I am confirmed in the maxim . . . that one must always work FOR Rome, sometimes WITHOUT Rome, never AGAINST Rome.*"

This is magnificently put, and it is no mere academic statement of an abstract idea. There is deep, personal experience behind every word. The maxim was forged from life, and was an excellent one for d'Alzon whose whole career was to be so identified with the interests of the Church that a peasant woman would later catch his whole character in a few simply spoken words : " When I see Father d'Alzon, I feel I am looking at the Church." D'Alzon had said of Lamennais that he was nothing without Catholicism. At that time, or at any other period of his life, he would have been as ready to say as much of himself : *Without the Church, d'Alzon is nothing.*

. . . . .

We have isolated and lingered over d'Alzon's part in this unfortunate affair, for it seems clear that this is the most important feature of his Roman period since it has the greatest significance in the story of his spiritual and intellectual formation. When in Montpellier, he had complained that he was being given " purely verbal knowledge " while he pined for the knowledge " of things and of facts." He certainly had his opportunity in Rome, and he certainly knew how to watch, weigh and learn.

The external facts of his Roman period are easily told. His father had asked him to lodge with a religious community " in order to live a more regular life ". There was, as so often, a great wisdom and the shadow of guiding Providence in this. In compliance with this wish, he took up residence with the Minims of *Saint Andrea delle Fratte*, in a room which, to his great joy, looked out on a garden of orange-trees. His studies comprised attendances at various public courses, and intense personal research. He wrote with great satisfaction to his father, that here he had the advantage of being permitted to attend the lectures of the best professors in different Universities, without being tied to any one establishment. At the end of four months, on the advice of several eminent men, especially on that of Father Ventura, he gave up attending public lectures and devoted himself to intense private work in his own cell. He was again, therefore, the solitary student he had been at Lavagnac, and he was able to set his own pace and pursue those " master ideas " which he considered so vitally essential for his " personal vocation ".

That cell certainly closed about him, and he resolutely kept to it. Rome could have been a place of seething distractions for him, for even the magnificent ceremonies had their horde of sightseers whose lack of reverence distressed him. In the University, he had turned away from the Jesuit professor who was floating about in some verbal lyricism of his own, of which d'Alzon gives this prime sample to his father : " And as regards eloquence, I find it useful to speak of painting, and painting brings me to Raphael, whose body was found a few months ago. Part the first : examination of the virtues and faults of Raphael. Part the second : examination of the works of Raphael. Peroration : relations between painting and eloquence. . . ." If this was a sample of what he heard at those public lectures, it was certainly a good thing that he abandoned them. He had not come to Rome to blow oratorical bubbles about eloquence and Raphael : it was not with foolishness like this that Europe would be shaken out of its torpor. In the same way, he turned aside from the liturgical functions in the Basilicas because he found himself ringed around by babblers and empty-headed sightseers. " *On Holy Thursday,*" he writes to his father, " *I went to ' Tenebræ ' in the Sixtine Chapel. I am no musician, but I knew that the ' Lamentations ' and the ' Miserere ' were magnificently rendered. However, the conduct of those around me was scandalous. They talked and talked . . . and I was extremely annoyed to find myself among people who regarded this ceremony as no more than a show. I did not go back again. . . .*" He also avoided useless visits. His visiting list had the names of those only with whom he could discuss those " master-ideas " which were his aim and his passion, so that d'Alzon could describe such visits as " dissertations rather than conversations ". " *When I go to visit Father Olivieri or Cardinal Micara or others of their calibre, I take care always to prepare any questions so that I may get their answers. I consult different people about the same question, so that I receive more light on the subject and am able to make more rapid progress."* He did not go to them for wit and wine and the conversation that fritters away time. When he came to them, they served him with wisdom for which he thirsted.

When he did find time to look at Rome, he saw the real greatness of Rome which appears only to the eyes of faith. *" In the two years I lived in Rome "*, he writes, *" it seemed to me that behind these ancient monuments, these Churches, these feasts, these masterpieces ; behind all this veil of magnificence which hides many other wonders from the eyes of the muddled and hurried traveller—I was able to reach the hidden significance of these venerable institutions, and to contemplate some of these men who have little concern for the world's applause and are content to be great and holy in the eyes of God."* It was this same thirst for the soul of things, that animated his studies, that directed his choice of friends. He has left us some very interesting pen pictures of these friends, and one of special interest on Cardinal Wiseman whom he was privileged to call his friend.

Time passed, and with it the priesthood came nearer. Some letters of his had been seized by the Austrian police ; and this, together with that ubiquitous gossip he hated and which had coupled his name so often with that of Lamennais, had led to his being suspect in high quarters of the Vatican. As a result, he was asked by the Pope to sign his personal adherence to the encyclicals against the doctrines of Lamennais before his admission to the Sub-Diaconate. This he did without the least hesitation, for indeed it was easy to renounce something which he had at no time accepted. At the height of his emotional crisis over the Lamennais affair, he had gone to St. Peter's and had kissed the feet of the Apostle's statue as a symbol of his submission and as a prayer for strength in submission. The Pope expressed his contentment. D'Alzon was pleased that His Holiness did so, though he could not resist adding : *" It is sad that this is the manner in which I have given satisfaction."* His heart still bled for his friend, and his prayers would follow him to the very end.

On December 26th, 1834, Emmanuel d'Alzon was raised to the priesthood. The first great period of his life was over, and " the needs of a world of men " were challengingly before him.

He rose and accepted that challenge magnificently.

THE FIRST CROWDED YEARS OF MINISTRY

AFTER HIS ORDINATION in Rome, Father d'Alzon came back to Nîmes. He found a sad state of affairs there. The diocese was without seminaries, since they had been either destroyed or sold; the Clergy, in the words of the aged Bishop of Nîmes, Mgr. de Chaffoy, were "scattered units" not knowing one another and each following his own lead; aspirants to the priesthood were few. The middle class was Protestant and Voltairean in outlook. In 1830, dormant religious passions had been whipped to fury by the removal of the crosses from public places, and the dust of conflict was still in the air. Vocations to religious Orders of Nuns were a thing of the past, and the communities had dwindled to nothing from lack of recruits. Schools and Catholic works were no more, except two or three that had been recently founded. Cholera had left its train of misery, and that misery had been exploited by corruption. In a word, the Church of Nîmes was in the dust. No one was more sorrowfully aware of this than the Bishop himself, and he looked forward with hope to the coming of Father d'Alzon, who could have chosen the diocese of Montpellier but who had decided for Nîmes. "Come then," Mgr. de Chaffoy wrote to him, "come to the aid of this poor diocese of Nîmes. . . .Come to the rescue of a poor old man and help him to bear a burden too heavy for his more than eighty years! We shall work together, we shall aid one another, we shall encourage one another to serve God to our utmost."

And yet, there was a certain embarrassment about his coming. What was to be done with him? You could not deal with such a brilliant young man as you would with an ordinary curate. Mgr. de Chaffoy solved his problem by appointing him honorary Vicar General. Eyebrows were raised in surprise at such a dignity bestowed on a young man of twenty-five in the first few months of his priesthood. One of the remarks made, according to M. Coudère, was the subtle one that " such favours belong to another age "—the age of nepotism; for the Vicar General, M. Liron d'Ayrolles, was the uncle of Emmanuel d'Alzon. Therefore . . . the eyebrows were raised and the shoulders were shrugged.

All this came to a head when an able and esteemed curate of the Cathedral stood up before a packed congregation and, in the presence of Father d'Alzon, made a direct allusion to the Bishop's choice. He spoke feelingly of the scandal of ambition in the very sanctuary, the scandal of those who " creep and intrude and climb " to the height of their ambition, using the dignity of their calling to reach power. It was a tremendous blow to Father d'Alzon—a pistol fired in his face, was his own description —but he made no complaint. This tall, handsome, aristocratic priest had suddenly appeared on the scene as honorary Vicar General. The good curate could see all that this implied of ambition, self-seeking, greed for ecclesiastical dignity; he could already see the haughty young priest lording it over all. . . . We would be less than just did we not appreciate his feelings, and less than merciful did we not forget those inflamed words from the pulpit, when, a few months later, the good curate came alive to the mistake he had made. For there was no haughty figure lording it over others. Instead—to the astonishment of the good man—there were swift and breath-taking glimpses of something redolent of St. Francis of Assisi : Father d'Alzon rushing through the streets with food hidden under his cloak for a starving family; Father d'Alzon quickly putting a dainty morsel from his plate into his napkin for some unfortunate: Father d'Alzon running after a beggar with the bread the poor man had dropped, and slipping it unobserved into his basket ; Father d'Alzon walking towards a raised pistol, till the mercy and compassion in his face opened the clenched fist of hatred in the poor wretch's heart, and another erring soul was won from the swirl of bewildered stupidity which is human sin.

For his coming to Nîmes was as the rush of blood to a sleeping limb ; it was felt everywhere. M. de Tessan is our testimony to the first few months, and it is clear from it that Father d'Alzon certainly came with such a rush of zeal to his work that he stirred the fears of even the least conservative. " From the beginning," he tells us, "Father d'Alzon showed a great zeal for virtue, an immense spirit of faith, devotion, and splendid sacrifice. Nevertheless, he was occasionally dizzy with his very activity, alive and too quick to act. He carried everything to excess, but his excesses were always occasioned by holiness or zeal though sometimes there was an admixture of temperament. Ah! what a magnificent example he has given! All that he was doing, was being done solely for the glory of God. . . ." Such was the studied impression of one who watched him closely.

The reaction of the poor and the wretched was more spontaneous, for they suddenly knew that a warmth had come into the cold places of their lives. They waited for him as he left the Cathedral, and he emptied his pockets for them. His old servant, Alexis, who came to look after his needs in those poor rooms in the *rue de l'Arc-du-Gras* knew this only too well, for it cost him many a headache. We find him running in distress (*Notes et Documents*, 11, 72) to his friend Madame Beauquier who kept the little wool shop in the *Arc-du-Gras*. "But you are joking, Alexis! You tell me you have not the wherewith to buy Father's dinner! That's impossible."—"Not at all," Alexis answered in a distressed voice, "*Father gives everything.* Money came from Lavagnac yesterday, but it's all gone. Father would give away even his shoes, if I were not there to stop him. All day they come seeking him, and *he always gives*. I have to borrow quietly from neighbours because there's nothing left . . ." Poor Alexis! Sometimes he had a very dainty bird for Father Emmanuel, and afterwards there was not even a bone left over. He certainly had not eaten the bones—and Alexis was left wondering what poor deserving wretch, or what scheming scoundrel, had had the benefit of his cooking.

Madame d'Alzon had something to say too about this 'frenzied' charity of her son. "*I believe*" he said, "*that the blessings of God are won by great sacrifices, above all when one seems to be completely emptying the coffers.*" But it did not stop at that. When the coffers were empty, there were his food, his boots, his clothes. Madame d'Alzon used to avail of his visits to Lavagnac to repair the ravages of his wardrobe caused by his headlong charity. Invariably, he would arrive darned and patched, he had given away everything. Madame would set vigorously to work ; and the poor of Nîmes would lie in wait for his return. We have the following from that delightful volume : *Sketches of Father d'Alzon* by his pupil and admirer, Father Galeran :

" One day, Father d'Alzon returned with a suitcase full of new linen, of splendid quality and marked with his name. His mother had done all this for her dear *pauper*. Among other things, she had put in a dozen pairs of black silk socks. The priest arrived home to Nîmes, to find as usual the empty hands of the poor stretched out to him. He had no money—and so he opened the suitcase and distributed all it contained. All the socks disappeared, and there remained only the empty suitcase to be filled anew. . . . A tattered beggar is said to have been seen near the *Maison Carrée* wearing magnificent silk stockings of which he was very proud and with which he would not part at any price. He was showing them to all and sundry, boasting whence they had come. Thus the poor were given the ' purple and fine linen,' while the Vicar General was content with the old and the patched. This, it was said, was extravagance and foolishness. Of course it was—and it is with such foolishness that the heights of wisdom are won. . . ." Father d'Alzon was incapable of keeping anything for himself except his worries.

There is a great impression of *swiftness* about this charity of his ; indeed, like Goldsmith's parson, his actions outstripped his conscious charity, for " his pity gave ere charity began." That same swiftness characterised all his actions. Even his spirituality was swift and watchful, for one of his fundamental principles was, in his own words : " *Seize the grace of God which lingers with you for a moment and may pass you by.*" Father Picard (*Notes et Documents*, 11, 39) gives us this vivid impression of Father d'Alzon under his full steam :

" He used to *run* from the Cathedral to his house, and back again. He seemed to be running even in the church. M. de Tessan reproached him with moving *like a storm*, vigorously displacing the chairs that happened to be in his way. Nevertheless, no one was surprised. . . . So much were his zeal, his fervent intentions, felt, that people became accustomed to seeing him running in the streets, hastening precipitately to sacristy or confessional. One day, however, after M. de Tessan's reproach, he reined himself in and walked in a very composed manner from one end of the Cathedral to the other, using the utmost precaution, displacing nothing. M. de Tessan saw all these efforts of his penitent, and knew that it just could not be. 'It makes you look like a pious hypocrite,' he said. 'It was not *you* any more. . . .'"

This need for the headlong was essential to his whole character. From the very beginning, he plunged into his work. He had come to Nîmes with two ideas : the conversion of Protestants, and the sanctification of the young. But he made his début with something quite different. His uncle, M. Liron d'Ayrolles, confided to him the direction of an Association known as the *Ladies of Mercy*. They were good ladies, given to charity, but aged and aristocratic ladies who could be querulous and exacting. The young priest faced up with some trepidation to his first sermon to this select little group—and it is sufficient to recall that he himself said afterwards : "*I felt I was swallowing handfuls of thorns all the time.*" But he got used to them, and he put new life into their languishing association. He was soon using the edge of his tongue on them for their own good, and they learned to take the truth from this priest who, unlike the others, was not awed by them. "*Mesdames,*" he is recorded to have said to them, "*you give yourselves in the morning to charity, and in the evening to the ball. Take care ! For some, that good work may well become the vestibule to hell. . . .*" And softening his severity, he would try a little salutary banter on the good ladies : "*Do you know why you are so generous ? You have a wardrobe which overflows and meals which are too lavish. . . .*" The truth was good for them, and they knew that there was a wealth of kindness below the thin surface of his severity. D'Alzon was certainly never cut out to be a benevolent director of old ladies, who must choose his words with polite circumspection. Nor had he any time for scented charity.

He was glad, therefore, when the opportunity presented itself of getting to the work of youth organization which he really wished to do. He took a room at the corner of the *rue de l'Arc-du-Gras*, and there began his *Society of Saint Louis de Gonzaga*.

He recruited boys between the ages of ten and fifteen years from the middle class and upper class of Nîmes society. His policy seems to have been to begin at the top and work down; for very soon we find him founding his *Society of Saint Stanislaus* for the children of the working classes. The aim was a double spiritual one: to prepare the younger ones for Holy Communion, and to help the older ones to persevere. He soon acquired an immense influence over these children. "They loved him wildly," we are told by many witnesses. There is a Peter Pan in every man of genius; a part of him that refuses to grow up, and gives him the insight to become a child among children. I remember calling on a learned Archbishop whose name was heavy with academic honours, and finding him at a school-children's party, crawling on his hands and knees and enjoying it. Father d'Alzon was like that. Once when Madame d'Alzon saw her "petit grand" as she called her son, racing about in the grounds at Lavagnac, dragging his cincture that the children might compete in catching it, she shook her head over him and said: "I just don't understand him". You really did, Madame —and if you did not, you should have asked the children. They knew, for he was a child among them.

In such a crowded life as his, it is necessary to hasten on to the picture of another d'Alzon—Father d'Alzon the confessor. He is not "running" now, he is not displacing chairs, he is not romping with his children; he is sitting still, hour after hour, in the Confession box, dispensing the mercy of the Christ he was serving so well. The confession box waited for every moment he could give it in his crowded day.

The programme of that day is amazing. He rose at half-past three or four in the morning, and made an hour's prayer before leaving his house. At 4.30 in Summer and 5 o'clock in Winter he celebrated Mass. This was done so punctually that we are told his sign of the Cross at the foot of the altar synchronized with the striking of the clock—for in this, as in everything else, d'Alzon was famous for his punctuality. After Mass, he "would run" to the confessional, and remain there till nine o'clock and then rush home to take a few mouthfuls of coffee (which he prepared himself, often scorching his fingers in his haste), in order to return to the Cathedral for the Office and the Chapter High Mass, which he never missed. Afterwards, he entered the confessional again and remained there as long as there was a penitent needing him. In the afternoon, when the Office in Choir was over, he returned again to his confessional, and remained there from 4 o'clock until 7 or 8, and even, on the eve of great feasts, until 11 o'clock. After that, when one would have expected him to take his ease, he went off to attend his reunions, or settled down to intense study. Somewhere in that crowded day there was a meal eaten with the utmost haste.

The people flocked to him, and the secret of his success was that this man who would scatter chairs in his impetuous haste could also turn calmly to each and very soul, giving his full personal attention as though life had no other concern for him. From the depths of his confessional, he began to renew the face of Nîmes. At the end of the day, he had moments when he felt staggered at the thought of the numerous Absolutions he had given. "I remember," wrote one of his penitents, "that once, on Holy Saturday, I went to the Cathedral for Confession very late. Father d'Alzon came from the sacristy towards me. He stopped, and, holding his head in his hands, he said to me: 'Pray to the good God for me, my child. I have given so many Absolutions to-day that I tremble to think of them!'" With every Absolution went his personal concern, so that every penitent knew that Absolution was something real and precious. Every penitent left with the impression that this good priest was interested in a wholly particular and exceptional manner, in his soul's welfare. Hence the secret of their flocking to him. "I have often looked at the crowd waiting, for three or four hours, their turn to kneel at his feet," wrote one of his penitents, "and I have often looked in wonder at their diversity. The working-class woman was side by side with the most distinguished lady; the most worldly side by side with the most pious and most prayerful maiden. His direction was big and enlightened, and he knew how to judge swiftly the dispositions of a soul. He was adept at giving a free impulse to his penitent, not by imposing his ideas, but by guiding you to accept his ideas according to the tendencies of your own character. He would take part in your interior struggles; and often, when a resolution had to be taken, he would halve the burden with you, he would offer a Mass for your intention, or he would say: '*I shall take the discipline for you, while you pray that you may know the Will of God.*' His favourite expression in such circumstances was: '*My child, I shall offer you up with Our Lord on the paten to-morrow.*' The fervour with which he said these words was irresistible. . . ." What a splendid testimony this is! It draws back the veil and shows us the real heart of this priest. It explains why he was called to the poorest wretches in the hour of final need: to a young man who had attempted suicide; to a person of high society whose repentance had been despaired of; to an obstinate Saint-Simonite about to face his God; to unnumbered waifs and strays of passion and stupidity, for whom the last sands of life's hourglass were running out. The cry was being raised with greater and greater frequency in Nîmes: "Send for Father d'Alzon." Send for the man who bends down towards you, and gropes for your soul's salvation as passionately as he would for his own.

"He would halve the burden with you. . . " So intensely did he seek these souls that when he met with weakness or with stubbornness to grace, or when he sought a special grace for a soul, he pleaded with his pain and his blood. It is fashionable to-day to look askance at 'the discipline' and to dismiss the holy man who uses it, with a few phrases of modern psychological jargon that explain everything. For modern psychology has not yet got round to considering, on spiritual grounds, the man whose heart is crucified with Christ and who wrestles with that Christ for the eternal soul. Father d'Alzon carried the weakness, the stubbornness, the hard crusts of ingrained habits, from the confessional with him; and the mark of his own blood on the whitewashed wall of his room was his answer and the signature of the price he was paying. We have many witnesses at all stages of his life, to the fact that his linen was constantly stained with blood; and we have the witness of his confessor, M. de Tessan, whose great concern was to moderate his penitent's heroic mortifications. Through the indiscreet words of Father d'Alzon's servant, Alexis, many details of his mortification were known. There were moments too when his burning anxiety for a soul caused him to cross the barrier of his secrecy. " There," he said vehemently to one of his penitents, more than usually recalcitrant to grace—" *There, that is what you are costing me !* " And he threw a blood-stained handkerchief on the table before her.

Yes, indeed, concern for the penitent did not end with the Absolution given. His words we have quoted from one of his penitents : ' I have given so many Absolutions that I tremble . . .' were grave words for him, because they meant : ' I have taken so many burdens on my shoulders and human weaknesses to my heart. . . .' The rest of the tale would be told to the sound of the scourge in that bare room of his, where maroon coloured oilcloth hung along the white-washed wall that the blood might not tell his secret by its stain ; where the only picture looking down from the bare walls, was one of the Magdalen weeping for his sins ; where the only sizeable piece of furniture was the big table with his books and manuscripts ; where the only ornament was a skull standing on the mantelpiece as a *memento mori* and as a comment, by this man born to earthly riches, on " the shows and all the fuming vanities of earth. . . ." When his confessor protested, he used to laugh with that light-hearted, infectious laugh of his, and say : " *Well, a good cook ought to taste all his dishes before serving them.*" He was asking his penitents to face their own weaknesses and vicious habits ; to struggle painfully towards grace, and to keep the heights of their personal holiness with pain. Along that road of pain, of struggle with self, he was determined to walk with them, and to exert all the strength of his spirit in shouldering the burdens of those who stumbled or fell. He would have none of their chalices pass by him without his tasting it. " *The sufferings of a priest are very beautiful,*" we have quoted him as saying, " *when they are considered, not as expiation, not as personal cross, but as sacrifice for others.*"

We now turn to that which he himself considered the most important matter in those years—his foundation of a Refuge for repentant Magdalens. The disruption of 1830, the pro-longed decadence of the Christian life in the diocese of Nîmes, cholera, industrial oppression, and general misery, had been "exploited in a frightful manner", as Father d'Alzon wrote in a letter to d'Esgrigny. Hence the darkness of sin, of want, of despair, and that swarm of poverty-stricken young girls exposed to the temptation of vice-money. Father d'Alzon was touched by their condition, and he set about doing something to alleviate it. With him, to think was to act—and so, Mgr. de Chaffoy found his newly-appointed Vicar General before him with an amazing request. In Rome, shortly after his ordination, Father d'Alzon had met that fine priest Father Feret, who had come to seek approbation for the *Institut des Dames de Marie-Thérèse*. Now, Father d'Alzon was asking permission to seek a community of these Sisters to found a *Refuge* in Nîmes.

He stood before the Bishop and he saw only the need and its remedy. The Bishop, however—aged and conservative—saw all the shadows that lay in the path of such a project. It was an undertaking very liable, he saw, to scandalize the pious, to irritate the impious, disquiet the good. There were absolutely no resources, and even if there were, these women would be only too ready to avail of all the charity they could get, and go their way, making a laughing stock of the Vicar General and his ideas. The good Bishop was very disturbed, for he knew that there was need for such an undertaking, and the young priest *on his knees* before him was pleading for a chance to do it. Finally, with an immense effort, Mgr. de Chaffoy took his eyes from the shadows, closed his ears for a moment to the clamouring voice of common-sense, leaned down to his Vicar and said: "My dear d'Alzon, all the holy founders have had one thing in common. They were all mad—and that quality you certainly share with them!" Thus, the hesitant permission was given, and when the young priest rushed off as though he intended to do it all before sundown, Mgr. de Chaffoy may well have sighed: "What next!"

He had no resources, and he set about collecting them. The Vicar General, for whose climbing ambition the good preacher had trembled in the pulpit, became a collector from door to door, a beggar of alms for charity. "*I am very busy,*" he wrote to his sister Marie, "*because I am begging through the town with one of the priests from the Cathedral. The story of our adventures would make a very curious novel. The number of poltroons and fools is astonishing!*" I think that delightful outburst was probably due, not to those who refused support, but to those wise men of 'the keen long faces' who accompanied their refusal with words of sage counsel. This was in August. By Christmas he has become so absorbed in the work that he writes to Lavagnac saying he simply cannot find time to come. "He is lost to us," Madame d'Alzon had written to her husband, with a little human annoyance and a great deal of spiritual joy. "He belongs to God." Slowly the funds were collected which allowed him to hire an old building, once an inn. It was to this that he brought the Sisters. They came to an almost empty, inconvenient house, and to a man who had little more than his burning zeal. It was enough, however, for these great pioneers. They loved him, for they recognized their own spirit in him, deep calling to deep. They called him *the Friend of the poor and of sinners, our Father in God*, and when he gave them as motto: Confidence in God and abandonment to Divine Providence—they accepted it with joy.

In spite of the apprehensions of the pious and the timid, the work got under way very quickly. "Repentant girls are crowding in from all sides," Father d'Alzon wrote. "God is blessing the work. . . ." They met with such warmth and charity that it more than compensated them for the hardships they had necessarily to endure in the beginnings of such a work. Father d'Alzon moved among them, gay and encouraging; playing games with them, throwing lumps of sugar in the air for them to catch; asking them who considered herself to be the worst among them, and giving a beautiful Rosary Beads to the girl who stepped forward; rushing to them with bounding joy when he had managed to collect a few francs for them. There was that magnificent moment when, under one of those splendid impulses of his, he turned to one of these street-women of yesterday and asked her to offer her life in place of that of the Mother Superior who was at death's door. The girl went before the Blessed Sacrament, and, in the Providence of God, her offer was accepted. "On the following day," read the annals, "she had a severe headache and was obliged to take to her bed. The Mother Superior, on the other hand, rapidly improved as the girl sank towards death. She knew that God was asking it from her ; she made no complaint, but prepared her soul for the sacrifice. Her *good Father* encouraged and sustained the girl to her last breath. Soon she gave up to God her soul, purified by immolation and by obedience. One of the last things she said was : " It is well. I may do evil, and the Mother Superior will do much good. . . ." Thus did beauty grow in the soil of those few years ; and the Magdalen came from her place in heaven to greet her sister in eternity. There were moments of sorrow too, in those first years, when the lure of the street proved too much, and some of the girls returned to their old haunts. That sorrow would be turned into joy when it happened that the prodigal sister returned. There was, for instance, the moment when one such returned just as they were acting a little play about the prodigal son. The play was abandoned for the real welcoming of a live prodigal. Again, there was the somewhat macabre incident of the libertine who pursued his repentant mistress to the very Refuge itself. The Mother Superior met him at the door, heard his arrogant request quietly, and asked him to return in ten days because she would not act without consulting Father d'Alzon. Her " good Father " must have known this repentant child of his ; he must have looked into her soul, with that strange piercing insight of his, and seen a weakness there that might cause her to succumb. He asked the girl to join him in a novena, " that God may remove every obstacle to your perseverance." On the third day of the novena, she became ill, and weakened rapidly. On the ninth day she breathed her last, tended with loving care by her Father and her Mother in God. " Before dying," we are told, " she made with all her heart, the sacrifice of what she had loved most in the world. She called the Mother Superior, and asked her to cut off her hair by which she had been chained to vanity and sin. . . ." Father d'Alzon had her body laid out in the parlour, surrounded by corpse candles and with the curtains drawn. When the young libertine arrived, as arrogant and as ardent as ever, Father d'Alzon asked him : " You still wish to see this young lady ? You are still determined to take her away?"—"Decidedly yes!"—The parlour door was opened, and he was shown in. . . . Father d'Alzon believed in an opportunely dramatic gesture to send a tremor through hardened souls.

The Refuge was to continue and flourish and be directed by other hands than those of Emmanuel d'Alzon. One of the big things about him was that, when he had taken infinite pains to plant and nourish the seeds of a good work he passed that work on to others to water and to reap the fruits. He had certainly sown his seeds of mercy in the Refuge; and its soil was already lovely with beauty—with the beauty of a girl who offered her life that the work might flourish, and with the beauty of another who repeated the gesture of Magdalen when she washed the Feet with her hair. . . . But in our story of these crowded years, we must reluctantly turn from it all, because there is so much to tell. Emmanuel d'Alzon was a man whose mind seethed with projects, and he spoke with regret of some of these "which I must renounce after having cradled them for a long time in my imagination." Works crowded on him, and yet it pained him, in the midst of their heat and their burden to renounce even *one* idea. Consequently, the writer gets the impression of about six men, "*striving to emerge from the skin*" (as he himself vividly put it in another context), of this Father d'Alzon, and feels the need of a volume on each of the six.

D'Alzon was pre-eminently a *priest*—that is to say, a man whose every action was motivated by the desire to forward the Kingdom of God, for whose service he had been consecrated and set aside. His immediate priestly action was double: from the height of the pulpit he influenced the *masses*, and in the depths of the Confessional he influenced *individuals*. His preaching alone was immense, and he did his congregation the courtesy of always preparing the notes for his sermons. It is significant for the whole trend of his life, that like Bossuet he began his preaching career with a sermon on the Immaculate Conception; for one of the fine thoughts that damask the writings of Emmanuel d'Alzon is this: "*Our finest book of spirituality and of mysticism is the Blessed Virgin.*" His preaching was doctrinal and practical; it was preaching from the heart

71

as well as from the head, and therefore it drew crowds to listen to him. He had learned from his experience in Rome, not to use the pulpit for the preaching of *self* in displays of learning and oratory. The young priest who came down from the pulpit after having delivered a very ornate sermon on the Passion, and who had the misfortune—or the good fortune, perhaps—to ask Father d'Alzon what he thought of it, learned this to his cost. "Come, my dear friend," was the answer, "there were more than one passion in your sermon. There was the historical Passion, told in your fashion ; there was your own passion, for you seemed very agitated ; and there was the passion of your congregation whom you detained beyond all reasonable measure. . . ." Another good priest thought to regale Father d'Alzon with an account of all the retreats, the sermons and the talks he had given, and he did so with a complacency which never failed to put a salutary edge of the language of Emmanuel d'Alzon.

"Ah, very good," replied d'Alzon, "but tell me something of the many subjects of these many discourses."

The good priest expounded at some length, and one can imagine that look in d'Alzon's eye which should have warned him that the whip was to ready be cracked.

"I am sorry," said Father d'Alzon, "that you have forgotten to preach a sermon on *intemperance of the tongue*."

Let us hasten to add, by way of an aside, that these salutary barbed words never made enemies of those in whose vanity they stuck. Their victims knew only too well the pure zeal of the man who spoke them, and they had every reason to know the kindness that came from that same source. D'Alzon had laid aside willingly all the worldly pomp and ceremony that could have been his by inheritance. It was too much to expect, therefore, that he should have been silently tolerant of pious pomposity or sugared piety. He was ready to laugh at what he would call a *petit curé de sucre*. It was the name of a little figure with a very benign, very sweet expression, that was common as a confection in the *Midi*, and as such he loved it. But when "the little sugar curé" met him in the flesh, he did not like it. "He hated devotional body contortions," writes

Father Galeran, " and he had a horror of fantastic devotions and vapours." Once when he had listened to the utmost verge of his patience to a priest who was weaving pious webs of language, d'Alzon ran a ruthless hand through the webs by saying :

" Father, let me know when you are going to take the Veil. I would like to preach at your clothing."

It will be immediately seen that a priest who brings such a forthrightness, such a clear preaching of Christ, to the pulpit, would be sure to win a following for his doctrine. For in the pulpit, nothing succeeds like sincerity, and people are quick to recognize and respond to sincerity. This was the secret of Emmanuel d'Alzon the preacher. It explains why he was asked to give so many Lenten sermons, so many sermons for special occasions, for special feasts. The enthusiasm aroused by his first course of Lenten Sermons in *Saint-Paul* (1836) reaches us through the columns of *La Gazette du Bas-Languedoc* : " We find it our duty to express, on behalf of the religious population whose organ we are, our gratitude to the young ecclesiastical dignitary whose zeal and devotion have been so keenly appreciated, and to our venerable Bishop whose choice, in very truth, heaven seems pleased to bless. . . ." According to the unanimous testimony from that time, scarcely a year had passed before this new apostle of Nîmes had already brought about a sensible transformation in the Catholic population and in all grades of society. " Already," he himself wrote to d'Esgrigny towards the end of 1837, " I am well on my way to being master of all the children of Nîmes aged from twelve to fifteen. In time, I hope to extend that influence to the older ones. Every year, I am gaining splendidly."

Perhaps the most effective way in which an impression can be given of Father d'Alzon's preaching is to quote from the testimony of those who heard him. " The language of Father d'Alzon," writes Mgr. Besson, " took on most lively colours suited to the subject on which he preached. In his discourses and his sermons, he was at one time firm and precise, at another rich and abundant, and again either outspoken or picking his words with caution. He would take the most sublime sentiments and considerations with matter that was unequal and sometimes too commonplace, but he was always able to lift himself again on the wing and to exalt his hearers with him to the heights of sublimity. . . ." Again, we have this tribute to his style from another priest : " Father d'Alzon, that man of action, had the Latin genius—strength and vigour. . . . His style was very much the man himself : strong, energetic, impetuous, sometimes familiar and often sublime. . . ." We could go on adding testimony to testimony, but let one more suffice. It is a tribute to Father d'Alzon's powers in circumstances which test the finest preachers—the preaching of a pastoral retreat. After one such, in speaking to his priests, Cardinal Pie said this of Father d'Alzon : " Hitherto, I have heard the chivalrous eloquence of the gentleman, the burning eloquence of the tribune, the unction-filled eloquence of the sacred orator, the simple eloquence of the apostle, the magisterial eloquence of the bishop. But in this retreat, I have heard them all together, and they have been successively splendid in the conferences of the priest who has preached to you and who unites all these qualities in himself. . . ." These quotations give an impression of the versatility and range of subject and of emotion on which Emmanuel d'Alzon could call. The important thing, of course, is that each of those successive voices of eloquence was also the voice of his burning sincerity.

Finally, we must glance at his work for the intellectual element of Nîmes. His whole background and intellectual upbringing had given him a high regard for the importance of the intelligentzia in the re-birth of religious life in France. Hence, from the very beginning, he held his " Mondays " when he was at home to all for the exchange of wisdom, not unseasoned with cigars and with punch. Nîmes had its generous sprinkling of mere conservatives—" rosewater Christians," as the local term so pleasantly described them ; but they did not come to *Les Lundis de M. d'Alzon*. The men who came were of the calibre of those two magnificent young men, Germer-Durand and Monnier, who were choice spirits nursing broken dreams in bitterness till they met with Emmanuel d'Alzon. These " Mondays " were meetings for vigorous philosophical and theological discussion, where young intellectuals sharpened their

brains against the whetstone of their opponents' arguments.
There was nothing stodgy about them—nothing pretentious,
nothing smug. For around those discussions flowed the free
stream of conversational charm, now serious, now bantering,
now quickening to a swirl of delightful nonsense bubbling with
free and healthy laughter. It all radiated from the central
figure, Father d'Alzon, who moved among his guests handling
out the punch he had mixed himself and the cigars to go with it.
The secret of his success with these men—and with all—was
that Emmanuel d'Alzon never believed that wisdom should walk
the world in a boiled shirt of pomposity stiffened with the starch
of a rather ridiculous high-seriousness. He knew how to wear
the full robes of seriousness when seriousness was called for ;
but he was quite ready then to don the motley of good humour
and good fellowship. Emmanuel d'Alzon was a man of the
utmost candour, the utmost disinterestedness, the utmost charm.
He was an aristocrat of nature and of grace.

We have seen d'Alzon the intent confessor leaning towards
a penitent as though his or her concerns were his sole concern
on earth ; we have seen him in the pulpit playing the whole gamut
of human feelings ; we have failed to keep pace with him in the
to-and-fro rushings of his headlong charity ; we have seen him
at home with the ignorant and at ease with the learned. It were
a pity, however, to miss one delightful moment of sheer high
spirits which Father Picard records for us. The scene is Mgr.
Chaffoy's palace, where His Lordship is speaking with Mgr. de
Prilly, Bishop of Châlons. Father d'Alzon is there too, taking
an able and comprehending part in the various discussions. A
nephew of the Bishop of Nîmes is also present. Soon some
question bearing on politics arises, and Father d'Alzon finds his
opinion at complete variance with that of the nephew. The
discussion gets warm, then takes a humorous turn. The two
challenge one another to a mock duel, and stretch out an arm to
serve as a sword. The " duel " is short-lived, for the Bishop
of Nîmes is in no mood for such pleasantries. He orders both
the young men out of the house. Father d'Alzon goes quietly
without a word. " That very evening," continues Father
Picard, "the Bishop, regretting his hastiness and the pain he

must have caused to Father d'Alzon whom he greatly loved and esteemed, sends him that magnificent crucifix with the Christ in ivory, which was to stand on Father d'Alzon's bureau. He offered it to him as a very humble reparation for the pain he had caused him . . . " The good Bishop need not have worried. Father d'Alzon was not a man who wore his dignity touchily on his sleeve. He was a humble man—or rather, that even more resplendent person, a very proud man who has learned humility. The whole incident gives us a flash of insight into the intimately human relations that existed between the Bishop and his young Vicar. The impression made by the whole conversation, including the mock-duel, on the other Bishop, Mgr. de Prilly, was perhaps surprising. So far from wishing Father d'Alzon out of his sight, he used every endeavour to persuade him to become his Coadjutor. Had Emmanuel d'Alzon been a small man, he could have accepted that dignity and thus have a small man's revenge for a slight. But he was a big man—a big man who, in Father Galeran's words, " made bishops, for he placed the golden mitre on more than one head ; but who chose the religious cowl for his own."

This is the story of the first few splendid and crowded years of Father d'Alzon's ministry. They contain sufficient for a whole lifetime's achievement, and are in reality but the beginning. " The activity of a priest," he had said at the beginning of his ministry—" The activity of a priest must not be confined within the four walls of the sacristy." And he had shown clearly in those few years just what he meant by that.

VICAR GENERAL OF NIMES

On September 29th, 1837, Mgr. de Chaffoy, Bishop of Nîmes, passed to his reward. He was eighty-six years old. His young honorary Vicar, Father Emmanuel d'Alzon had been privileged to raise his hand for the last time in absolution over him, for Father d'Alzon had been in constant and loving attendance on his Bishop in his last years. Now he was chosen by the Chapter to preach the Funeral Oration—an honour which shows, as perhaps nothing else does, how high an opinion his fellow-clergy had of his preaching. At that particular moment, a thousand matters were clamouring for his attention, and we have his own words for the fact that he had only a few hours he could devote to composing his oration. We shall dwell on that oration, both as an example of his style and as a proof that this " fiery priest " could pick his way truthfully, fearlessly, and with the utmost tact, through a situation delicate to the point of being thorny. A conventional eulogy full of abstractions and floweriness, would of course have been an easy solution ; but Emmanuel d'Alzon was not the man to take an easy solution ; his sincerity would not allow of words whose only merit was that they avoided an issue.

There were two issues. The first concerned the life of the Bishop himself. His episcopal reign had been a long and troubled one which he had dominated by the sheer power of his gentleness and moderation. In 1830, those lovely crucifixes some eighteen feet high, which can be seen today at the back of the Cathedral and Saint-Perpetue in Nîmes, stood in the public places. In the religious disturbances of that year, by order of the civil authorities the crosses were removed. The Catholics, goaded to exasperation, were banding themselves to take forcible measures, when their Bishop came among them and calmed them. This was, in a sense, the highlight of his reign, but it presented a problem. The congregation before whom the oration was to be given would contain many Protestants, and therefore a reference to such "old unhappy far-off things" might be considered highly imprudent. On the other hand, omission of this would be a significant gap in the Bishop's life-story, the story of a man of meekness which omitted the greatest triumph of his meekness. D'Alzon was not a man to shirk the issue.

The second thorny patch concerned the Vicar General, M. Laresche. He had come from Franche-Comté with Mgr. de Chaffoy, and the latter had made several unsuccessful attempts to have him named as Coadjutor. From the very beginning, M. Laresche does not seem to have been popular with the clergy of Nîmes, and in the last years of the Bishop's life, Mgr. de Chaffoy left matters more and more in his hands. His decisions were not popular, and at the time of the Bishop's death, he had reached the nadir of his unpopularity. Now the Chapter had matters in its own hands, and the muttering against M. Laresche which had long been apparent, would certainly take the form of open and determined opposition. If Father d'Alzon had been a man who prudently consulted his own immediate interests, here indeed was a subject to be avoided, or if included, then worded in such a way that there would be implied criticism to please the powers that now held sway. Father d'Alzon knew M. Laresche better than any of his hearers, and he knew those unpopular decisions of his from the inside. We do not know what he really thought of many of those decisions ; he made it clear, however, that he considered M. Laresche an upright man who was prepared to stand between the Bishop and his pastors and take the lash of criticism and calumniation. This was how Emmanuel d'Alzon saw the matter ; this was how he would present the matter ; and let cowardice wear its mask of " prudence," but he would have none of it. The young priest determined therefore, to pay a warm, personal, truthful tribute to the great Bishop whom he had loved so well, and respected so deeply. From his very first words, it was clear that he was not going to pay a cold impersonal tribute, nicely trimmed to the supposedly tender feelings of all.

" The Lord has sanctified him because of his faith and his meekness ! " he quotes from *Ecclesiasticus*, and he continues :

Father de Tessan pressed the matter, and discovered that the Bishop was afraid he himself would be jealous. Here we have the secret of the Bishop's constant hesitancy : in any decision, he saw round the next corner where someone was licking a wound, or where some resultant disaster lurked. Father de Tessan protested that this was not so at all. " Here again," writes Mgr. Besson in his *Vie de Mgr. Cart*, "he was drawing the inspiration for his choice from the ideas of his predecessor . . . The future was to justify fully all the hopes which Mgr. Cart had put in Father d'Alzon . . . "

But they were strange yoke-fellows, the ardent impetuous young d'Alzon with his fearless adventurousness, and the cautious *nisi quod traditum* Mgr. Cart who tersely summed up their relations in the words : " He will urge me forward, and I shall rein him in." That Father d'Alzon felt that rein sorely was very soon apparent, but his submission never wavered. " I see," the Bishop said to him very shortly after his appointment, " that you and Father de Tessan are very friendly, and this disturbs me. I do not wish you to be friendly to that extent, because the secrets of administration might involuntarily slip out in your conversation . . . " The hint of suspicion here hurt the young priest deeply. But, with that frank and open nature of his, he went straight to Father de Tessan and told him of the Bishop's wish. " From that day," writes Father de Tessan, " there was a coolness between Father d'Alzon and me." It clearly caused great distress to both, but his Bishop's wish for Father d'Alzon was the command of the Church he was vowed to serve—and that was that.

By the end of 1839, there was a delicate situation about his beloved *Refuge*, as we learn from an intimate letter to his sister :

" I have had a peck of trouble these last few days. The Bishop has refused to recognise the conditions of relationship with the *Dames de Marie Thérèse*, as accepted by Mgr. de Chaffoy. All that was to be cancelled. The Mother General has come, and the affair has been settled. But it has all been painful. I had made it clear to the Bishop that since he would not recognise propositions agreed to verbally, I would have no part in the discussion of a new arrangement. However, since the Mother

General who, I know not why, swears only by me, begged me to represent her, I undertook to bring the two parties to an agreement. Anyhow, this shows the difficulty which the best intentioned people meet with in trying to do good . . . "

"I made it clear to the Bishop . . . " These words show very clearly, as the whole relations between him and his Bishop show, that while Emmanuel d'Alzon was ever humbly submissive, he was certainly not an episcopal " yes-man " who would have been utterly useless as Vicar General. The whole passage is filled with overtones of strain. Pieyre, the historian of the town of Nîmes, remarks that on the day Father d'Alzon was appointed, the first locomotive steamed into Nîmes, and he seems to imply a symbolical connection between the two events in the sense that, with the coming of d'Alzon, " steam was to replace the merovingian carriage " in diocesan administration. Reading a passage like the one we have quoted, however, gives us an idea of how th wheels of that metaphorical " locomotive " d'Alzon were kept spinning in one place, while the episcopal hand on the controls hesitated again. But Mgr. Cart had his worries too, for he was not at all anxious to be the dark shadow in the path of d'Alzon. How revealing are those anxious words which he wrote to his secretary : " Father d'Alzon has written to me from Lavagnac. He says he is tired of twiddling his thumbs, that he is returning to Nîmes to carry into effect certain projects which he has been meditating during his rest. My dear friend, let us take to our prayers ! He will come to us with some new work he wishes to found, and he will fling himself into it with his usual fire. We shall not be left long in peace—everything will be set in motion . . ."

It would be no exaggeration to say that, when Mgr. Cart found peace disappearing around him, he may well have prayed : " From the fiery d'Alzon deliver me." If in a human moment, he may even have admitted such a thought, the Lord was deaf to the prayer because there were mighty things waiting for that fire of Emmanuel d'Alzon. Meantime, as Father Vailhé remarks (*Vie* 1.268), " by the contrary pull of these two temperaments, things sometimes remained at a standstill, neither advancing nor going back."

This was the "public portrait," so to speak, of Mgr. Cart; but there was also the private person, the Bishop whose gentleness and priestly courtesy sent some people away thinking of St. Francis de Sales. He quickly won the affection and esteem of his priests, for whom Father d'Alzon was the mouthpiece when he said to his Bishop with charming frankness: "Monseigneur, you may have your faults, but they are compensated for by three advantages. Your heart is a tomb of secrets; you respect your priests as no one else respects them; and you are a saint." Here, behind the public "pull of temperaments" lies the secret harmony between two men who appreciated one another to the full. "Father d'Alzon is a man of God and a man of power," is Mgr. Cart's studied opinion of him. The natural frigidity which existed at first between men of such contrasts, quickly thawed when they made a journey together to Franche-Comté in 1843. He told his Bishop how, having devoted himself to his service for a year, he began to think that Mgr. Cart did not understand his affection and thought him "too forward . . ." "As a result," he continues, "I was somewhat irritated until my journey in Franche-Comté, when you offered to accept my resignation if, having consulted your friends, M. Thiébaud and M. Doney, I was not convinced that what I had regarded as personal to me was really your ordinary natural conduct. Henceforward . . . my affection for you was again completely restored . . ." It is splendid that we can eavesdrop on these two men of God, and see how the saints make up their differences. In recording this conversation in a letter to Mère Marie-Eugénie de Jesus, however, Father d'Alzon has a significant aside. After the words "my affection", he adds in brackets—"I did not say to him *my confidence*." He was too truthful to give the impression that the public uphill struggle against the slope of the Bishop's hesitancy, and his own refusal— this side obedience—to leave the locomotive and re-board the merovingian carriage, were not to go on. Once again, as always, he would "stand even while he knelt."

In spite of these vexatious thorns in his path, Emmanuel d'Alzon continued his pioneer work in many directions. Under the drive of his inspiration, schools were founded in many places, and religious communities were established in some parishes, for example the Christian Brothers of De La Salle came tò Le Vigan, the Ursulines to Sommières, the Soeurs de Saint-Joseph to Nîmes and so on.   In 1836, the Sisters of Charity opened an independent school in Nîmes.   In 1840, again at the request of Father d'Alzon, the same Sisters opened an adult school for girl workers and domestics who had no other means of instruction.   Classes were held very early in the morning, before these young girls and women set out for their shops and factories.   Father d'Alzon was helped by a Father Privat who later made this admission : " I believed that we were rash and even a little foolhardy to undertake this school for adults.   I wished to discourage Father d'Alzon, but I see that I was wrong.   Two hundred crowded immediately to these lessons, and mothers accompanied them too."

It would take us beyond the scope of this book to enter into any further details of Father d'Alzon's ministry.   The general picture must suffice, of a hungry energy that reached out to everything that could forward the Kingdom of God, that met every problem with a vigorous solution.   The secret of his success was that he gave himself to the full.   Mgr. Cart used to refer, for example, to the *predicomania* of his Vicar General ; and the Vicar General used to answer those prudent voices that counselled moderation : Bah ! If the preacher is not exausted at the end of a Lenten course of sermons, he has made no conversions." The spirit he expressed here was typical of everything which he undertook, but it must not be thought that there was anything superficial about such a multitude of works.   He laid down the foundations of each thoroughly, and only then did he leave each more or less to its own resources.   " I act as the hens do," he wrote.   " When their chickens have grown, the hens give them a few pecks to drive them away on their own, and then they turn to others who need them."   This is one image for his work ; but another necessary image is that of an intellectual, radiating beacon giving heat and light to choice souls.   Monnier and Germer Durand knew that light and that heat ; the historian M. Gemain knew them ; the poet Reboul thrilled to them and wrote his splendid *Meditation religieuse et poetique sur la Croix* ;

and many others too who, at this time and at every other period of his life, looked to Emmanuel d'Alzon for inspiration and found him, as it were, a mirror of Christ. He had a genius for directing choice souls, and one of the first to come his way was the magnificent Eugénie Milleret, Foundress of *the Nuns of the Assumption*, to whose rescue he came when she had got into difficulties with that brilliant, prolific, but somewhat erratic genius among the French Clergy of the nineteenth century— Father Combalot.

The relations between Emmanuel d'Alzon and Father Combalot date from the early years of Lavagnac, when the d'Alzon children used to refer to him intimately and affectionately as *Papa Combalot*. When Father Combalot began to enthuse over this twenty year old girl who was so good, so distinguished, so clever that after three months' study she could translate Virgil "with astonishing accuracy"; and when he told him she was already wearing a purple dress which would soon be replaced by the purple habit of the Congregation he was going to found with her "for the regeneration of society through woman"; when eventually, Father Combalot had swept him off to hear this prodigy of his translating Virgil, Father d'Alzon's initial doubts became a certainty. Father Combalot had been nursing this idea of a new Congregation for many years. He had the insight to recognize that the young Eugénie Milleret had the stuff of a Foundress in her, and Father d'Alzon realized that too; but Father Combalot did not recognize what Father d'Alzon saw only too clearly—that he himself had not the stuff of a Founder in him. " I then knew this good Father Combalot very intimately," he was later to write, " and from certain points of view I had no longer any confidence in him as a *practical man*." Whenever he met him, Father Combalot was full of plans that took him in a dozen different directions within a short time. Hence the humour in this little exchange when they were discussing the project:

D'Alzon : My dear Father, I believe this project is quite feasible, and I am intensely interested in it. But I see only one obstacle . . .

Combalot : And that is ?

D'Alzon : Yourself. You must know how important it is for such an undertaking that you should direct it yourself personally in the first few years ?

Combalot : But I shall not be leaving Paris for at least four years !

D'Alzon : Well, I am going to Valence to preach a Lenten course. Will you come ?

Combalot : Certainly.

D'Alzon : Well, you can judge from that how secure I think your foundation will be ! You were not going to leave Paris for four years a minute ago, and now you are already running to pack your bags !

The story that centres around Father Combalot and Mère Eugénie belongs to another place. Mère Eugénie gives us this account of its humble beginning : " On April 30th, 1839, the Feast of St. Catherine, led by Providence, without really knowing just where it was directing us, the first religious of our Congregation had come together in Paris in a little room . . . These were Sister Marie-Augustine and myself. I was twenty-one years old, and she was twenty-two." The inevitable soon happened. Father Combalot had not the patience for detail required of him, and he was attempting to rule the new Congregation with a hand that reached towards it vaguely from afar, and through a multitude of other things. Difficulties between the Founder and his Daughters developed rapidly and became chronic. " To give full due to the action of Divine Providence," wrote Mère Eugénie, " it must be agreed that the character of the holy priest who guided us must certainly render the accomplishment of his designs something like a miracle. God had given him great gifts : he had received the grace of real illumination on the mystery of Christ ; he had a great love for Our Lord, for the Most Blessed Virgin and for the Church ; he had the spirit of faith and he was permeated with the Christian spirit ; he was a lover of poverty and simplicity. But to these fine qualities were added none of those which are necessary to government. Wisdom, patience, perseverance, a feeling for order and hierarchy were qualities quite opposed to his character, and moreover it was universally known in the Church of France that he lacked these qualities . . ." How painful must have been this position for her, at the mercy of a man of zeal indeed who would cast fire on the earth but who would not wait to tend that fire ! Relations between them became more and more strained. In the Autumn ot 1840, she asked to be allowed to consult another priest on her problems, and she put forward the names of all his friends without success. Finally she mentioned Father d'Alzon. " Emmanuel d'Alzon ? Oh yes, yes ! You may write to him as much as you like." Thus began a series of letters which show Father d'Alzon's genius for spiritual direction, and the fine, intelligent receptivity to all that is best and most noble which marked the soul of Eugénie Milleret with the seal of spiritual greatness.

It was inevitable that very soon Father Combalot should look on Mère Eugénie as one who had stepped out of line with him, to stand between him and his work. He decided to remove all his nuns from Paris to Brittany—except the Mother Superior who was to be left to her own resources. The Sisters, however, refused to break with their Foundress, and brought their cause before the Diocesan Council of Paris. Father Combalot then tried direct appeal to the Sisters, but without success. With a generosity that was characteristic of him, he wrote a fine letter to the Archbishop accepting the state of affairs, and commending his work and his Daughters to his Lordship's protection. Father Gros was immediately appointed Superior.

This sudden departure of the Founder made the Foundress feel somewhat left in the air. Those who succeeded him could not possibly know with proper intimacy the ideas which inspired the foundation. She turned to Lacordaire, to de Salinis, to Gerbet, to Rauzan ; but all of these had too much to do already. " In the designs of God," read the *Annals*, " it was Father d'Alzon who was to be the staff, the guide and the support of the Foundress. He had grasped the idea underlying her work, the good which was in her ; and he was happy to put all that he had of zeal, of intelligence and of devotion, to the service of a friend called by God to effect great designs . . . So far from being deflected from its aim by a change of spiritual director, the Assumption found itself impelled more energetically than ever towards the realization of its ideals. It is impossible not to see here again an intervention of Providence . . ." Mère Eugénie found in him all those qualities which were lacking in Father Combalot. In one of his articles, Father d'Alzon has this to say of Cardinal Newman: " As he ascended, vast horizons opened before his eyes; but he knew also how to descend, gently and effortlessly, to the exact examination of details." These words, as Mère Eugénie soon discovered, could have been written of himself.

In October 1844, she came from Paris to Nîmes, and together they discussed the final form of the Constitutions. I have been shown the path where they paced together for hours, discussing, pausing to make a note, standing for a moment to decide something, pacing again. Where I stood there was a magnificent mass of flowers just above my head. The French call it " the Passion flower," for it contains in a most remarkable fashion the shapes of all the instruments of the Passion. I thought of these two chosen souls, and how suitable it was that I should have found that flower in the place where they walked. For they carried in their hearts the image of the Crucified as the pulsating centre of all that they thought and did. So ardently did Mère Eugénie appreciate what Father d'Alzon meant to her and to her work, that at his death in 1880 she wrote to Mgr. Besson: " He was truly our Founder and our Father. We have never ceased to give him that name, and his death leaves us orphans."

The fine spiritual friendship between Father d'Alzon and Mère Eugénie would receive, in a more comprehensive treatment of Father d'Alzon than we can give within our limits, its adequate emphasis as of the splendour which marked the relations between St. Francis and St. Clare, St. Francis de Sales and St. Chantal, Father Pernet and Mère Marie de Jesus, and the other pure flowers of spiritual union which have been sources of such strength to the Church.

But we must again turn the page, for there are many events clamouring for their place in his story. What Flaubert (*Lettres*) said of Shakespeare is true, in another context, of d'Alzon: " He was not a man, but a continent, for there were great men in him . . ." We can but look ahead of us, and tell the story of the next peak of achievement that arises in the " continent " that was Emmanuel d'Alzon. For were we to treat any one achievement of his career with all the rich detail it deserves, we would reach the limits of our space and still be somewhere on his first peak. If ever a man could write the Petronian *Pervixi—I have lived*—on every moment of his life, that man was Emmanuel d'Alzon.

THE PEAK OF HIS ACHIEVEMENT

In spite of the myriad undertakings which claimed every ounce of his energy at every moment of his career, the clear line of inner development with Father d'Alzon is towards the Religious Life. We have seen him come to the very verge of this Life, but he hesitated there uncertain what his choice should be among the many Orders and Congregations whose spirit and characteristic way of perfection spoke their word of challenge to him. He could not hear the exact word for which he listened. In every action of his life there surged those inspiring words : *Adveniat Regnum Tuum.* The time had come when the inspiration of those words would become incarnated in a new Congregation founded by Father d'Alzon. It was characteristic of the man that, while he wished to become a religious, he founded the congregation in which he would become a religious. We have met d'Alzon the student, d'Alzon the friend of Lamennais, d'Alzon the preacher, d'Alzon the confessor, d'Alzon the friend : now it is time to introduce yet another d'Alzon—another of the " great men in him "—d'Alzon the Founder. The rest of the life-story of Emmanuel d'Alzon comprises largely two achievements : the foundation of the Fathers of the Assumption, the peak of his achievement ; and the foundation—with which we shall be especially concerned—of the Oblates of the Assumption, the crown of his achievement, the spiritual child of his maturity and his experience.

It is with keenly whetted interest, therefore, that we turn to the definition of a Founder which Father d'Alzon gave and which must have represented the ideal at which he himself aimed. " *What is a Founder?* he asks. And he answers : " *When God wills to mould and shape a Founder, He takes a man and He fashions him after the manner of the patriarchs. He prepares him from afar ; He fills him with His spirit ; He gives him a clear intuition of what He wishes from him, and what mission He has given him.*

Towards this end, He sets his heart aflame, He strengthens his desire by directing that desire towards an end which is at first realized in a dark manner, but which gradually emerges into the light through the action of supernatural clarities. God adds wisdom, holiness and paternity. Wisdom that he may choose the proper means, that he may formulate rules and constitutions ; holiness that he may be an example, " forma gregis " ; paternity or fecundity that he may have many spiritual sons to co-operate in the work and to perpetuate it . . . God has saved the world through His Son, and He has been pleased to join therewith the co-operation of the Immaculate Virgin. The Son perpetuates His work through the Apostles and their successors in the Church. The special and extraordinary missions confided to the Founders of Orders are continued by their disciples, always within the Church, always under the authority of the Supreme Pastor . . . "

This, then, is the inner drive which led Father d'Alzon to establish his Fathers, and this too is the spiritual picture of d'Alzon the Founder. He had indeed been prepared " from afar " when the thought of devoting himself " to the defence of religion " had taken shape in his young heart " in an amazing way " ; the spirit of God had taken fiery possession of him so that he brought the strength of ten to the task before him ; he had written on his standard the words *Adveniat Regnum Tuum*, as the expression of a man who stands before his God with arms flung wide to embrace any work that might be asked of him, and now those words were to come to full life in his years as the inspiration of his Congregation : the Fathers of the Assumption. The " clear intuition " he received of the mission given to him was the reward of many years of enthusiastic devotion.

It was the educational needs of the times that led Father d'Alzon to establish his Fathers of the Assumption. All through his career, he was keenly interested in the educational question, and was in the vanguard of those who were fighting for freedom of Catholic schools and colleges and recognition for them on a par with State schools. The chain of events which led to the foundation of his Congregation, may be said to have begun with a letter he received in 1843 when he was enduring, as best his impatiently active nature could do, a period of rest with his Bishop in Franche-Comté, It came from Father Goubier, the parish priest of Saint-Perpétue in Nîmes, and brought the news that he had purchased, in their joint names, the educational establishment founded by Father Vermot. The price was 78,000 francs, to be paid in ten years at five per cent—and as a further detail of interest to Father d'Alzon, his correspondent told him that he hadn't a penny! This was the way things happened in the life of Father d'Alzon. He probably chuckled at the sheer audacity of the undertaking, but he did not flinch from it—for it was just the sort of " crazy " step he found worked out best in the end. If there is one thing more than another which emerges from the material history of the foundation of religious Orders, it is that to be without visible resources seems to be an essential pre-requisite !

Father Vermot was a priest of the diocese of Besançon, and was brought into the Nîmes diocese by his compatriot, M. Laresche, the Vicar General. There seems to have been a remarakable similarity between Father Vermot and Father Combalot, in this respect at least, that they were both holy and zealous men, but both lacking in that perseverance in hammering out details and in remaining at the scene of activity which should go hand in hand with a spirit of enterprise. Thus, once again, Father d'Alzon was being called upon to take the helm of a ship which another had launched bravely but had allowed to drift towards the shallows. Father Vermot had brought an establishment and had built extensions to it so as to convert it into a boarding-school, but so haphazardly and with such little thought for design that it came to be popularly known as " Noah's Ark." He set vigorously about the task of getting pupils, and in 1838 had a fine roll-call of 150 as a promising start to the work he had undertaken. We are not concerned here with the details of the next five years, but only with the fact that when this letter reached Father d'Alzon in 1843, the roll-call at the *College of the Assumption* had dropped to twenty. Discipline was poor, and the remnant of that once promising venture was just something to be pointed out with disdain by the State University authorities as clear evidence that such " free " enterprises by the Church in the field of education were doomed to failure through sheer incompetence.

Meantime, through Father d'Alzon, a convent of Carmelite nuns was established just opposite the College. For some reason, this seemed the final straw to the students, who came near to rioting and cried out : " We don't want to be turned into seminarists or Carmelite nuns ! " And it was into this hubbub that the tall, commanding figure of Father d'Alzon burst, to re-establish order and to take up the challenge of Christian education. A short time previously, an eminent ecclesiastic had written to Father d'Alzon : " I spend my life looking for *men*. You can imagine, Monsieur, what satisfaction it is to me when I meet with one . . ." This was the impact of d'Alzon on the pupils too; they felt the vigour and the virility, the manly forthrightness that went out from him, and their answer was soon given in the improvement of their conduct and in the new spirit that entered into the College of the Assumption.

" There are two ways of governing men," said Pope Leo XIII. " You can govern them with a hand that hides in a heart, or with a heart enclosed in a hand." Father d'Alzon's was the first method : you knew the warmth of his heart, but at the same time you felt a firm hand there to meet your weaknesses and to chastise your failures. " Two characteristics were happily joined in him," writes Canon Galeran, one of his pupils. (*Croquis* p.47). " He was the father of the family and the commander of an army." With that eagle eye for which he was famed, he quickly singled out and sent away those who were the incorrigible sources of disturbance—and only teachers who have had to face up to a similar task will realize just how much this implies ; then he set about moulding the others according to a new pattern— the d'Alzon pattern, for which the College was to become famous. How successful he was in handling these boys is seen from the tributes which the writer, Ernest Daudet, paid to him : " All his pupils loved him passionately."

The picture we assemble from a hint here and an anecdote there, of d'Alzon the professor, is one of kind firmness which sometimes blossomed into a warm kindness in a word spoken or a gesture made. On the one hand, he would strike vigorously and sternly at anything which threatened discipline, as when he summarily cancelled out of existence a College musical band whose members had shown disrespect to the Prefect of Discipline ; on the other hand, when he had occasion to reprove a pupil for a fault, he balanced his sternness by pointing out the good qualities in the boy which should be sufficent to overcome this fault, and this sent him away reproved but encouraged. " He treated his pupils," writes Father Galeran, " in a manner which inspired in them a profound idea of their own personal dignity." He treated them as *men* who were proud to accept discipline, and who, when a fault was sternly pointed out to them, were also made to feel that they had within themselves the resources of their own manliness, the ability to shake themselves free and stand upright. All this was felt from that very first moment in 1844, when, as one of the pupils tells us, the refectory door was shot vigorously open, and a tall priest stalked in : " Gentlemen, this house is mine. At this moment, I have the honour of having you dine under my roof. You will please pack your bags, go home to your families and not return here—with the exception of three to whom I shall speak individually . . ." That was the beginning. The reign of anarchy was over, and that of discipline had begun in no uncertain manner. As ever more and more pupils came to what was really a completely new college under the old name, they learned to love that hand of discipline which expressed such geniune love for them, and such sincere concern for their interests.

Many tributes have been paid to the clear and vivid lessons— particularly in Church history—which Father d'Alzon gave to his pupils. But to show how well he could speak to boys, we shall select a passage from a sermon he preached to them, and which has been preserved for us by Father Galeran. It had indeed an *ex abrupto* opening calculated to jolt boys into attention when they had settled themselves in comfortable expectation of " the usual " :

" Gentlemen, have you ever seen Father Mattan, the late lamented parish priest of Saint-Baudile ? Father Mattan was very ugly. A nose, or rather a rubicund bulb, blossomed on his round, tomato-coloured face, and two little black gimlet eyes seemed to pierce the flesh, all this being crowned with white, unkempt hair, half-disciplined by an old leathery skull-cap. This is an exact picture. What do you think of it? Well then—I tell you frankly that I have several times seen this priest when he prayed, especially during his thanksgiving; I have gone on my knees as close to him as I could and at an angle to him, in order that I might contemplate the beauty of that face and the holiness of its expression. I witnessed a real transfiguration. I then recalled to mind certain faces I knew, perfect faces for the painter's brush, with regular features and due proportions; and these faces had nothing to say to me, and I no longer saw them as lovely. Why? Whence came this beauty? . . . True beauty is the reflection of the soul. The greater the perfection of the soul, the more beautiful becomes the exterior expression. At the resurrection, our bodies will be transformed in direct proportion to the transfiguration of our souls . . ." A priest who could speak in this virile manner to boys was certain to hold his audience.

At this point in our story, we find ourselves turning more and more to Father Galeran's splendid *Croquis*, for he gives us lively first-hand accounts of those early years in the College. He tells us how constantly that part of the College known as "Noah's Ark" was being changed. "The history of Jerusalem, a city eighteen times razed and re-built, can alone give an idea of the changes undergone by the ark'. . . . It seemed the ambition of every prefect of discipline to be its Nebuchodonosor." Through the *Croquis*, we are able to open Father d'Alzon's door and walk in, because sometimes, when the stomach pains from which he habitually suffered were especially severe, he would call young Galeran and ask him to sweep and tidy his room. Normally he did so himself. This enables us to get a description of " this real monastic cell with its whitewashed walls " :

" On the left as you entered was the bed, composed of two trestles, three planks, a very hard straw mattress, a stuffed bolster and a straw pillow . . . On the right, facing the bed, was a table of white deal on which there was a crucifix, a statue of the Blessed Virgin, and a skull. Besides these articles, there were a small chest of drawers, and a bed-side table similar to those in the dormitory. Above the chest of drawers was a small three-shelved library containing some works of piety, among them a

Bible, the *Confessions of Saint Augustine*, Cardinal Bona's *Treatise on the Sacrifice of the Mass*, a fine Elzevir edition of the *Imitation*, and a number of books of the Rules of different religious Orders."

All this combined to make d'Alzon a hero for his boys : the fine figure and military bearing, the crisp words whether of instruction or of command, the obviously keen interest in their welfare, and the austerity of that room which told them that this was no mere man of words, and which some of them must certainly have contrasted with the grandeur of Lavagnac that might have been his. In itself, the story of Father d'Alzon the Professor is of great interest ; but we must now study that College of the Assumption from another angle, as the centre and focus for the foundation of a new Congregation in the Church. Those books of the Rules which young Galeran saw, were very significant indeed.

We can mark some definite points in the growth of d'Alzon's idea of a new Congregation. One day, when he was celebrating Mass before the miraculous image of the Blessed Virgin at the Sanctuary of the *Consolata* in Turin, he took a vow to serve God all his life as a simple priest and to refuse, except the Pope should order him, to accept any ecclesiastical dignity. Immediately he felt himself urged, as by an inspiration of heaven, not only to embrace the life of perfection, but to found a religious Congregation. This he revealed to the Marchioness de Barole, a very remarkable woman. It was the " clear intuition " for himself which he laid down in the abstract when he defined a Founder. Another important factor was the encouragement and the urgings he received from that great spiritual soul, Mère Marie-Eugénie de Jesus. She begged him to found an exclusively teaching Congregation, the male counterpart to her own. While he was uncertain as to what the aims of his Congregation should be, he was unwilling to restrict it. He had laid down as its " new base " that it should be characterized by : (1) *the acceptance of all that is Catholic ;* (2) *candour ;* (3) *liberty.* The aims of his Congregation would have a similar broad sweep in them. " I am ready to do what God wishes and all that He wishes. But what does He wish ? I am in profound darkness as to the answer." But he was soon to give that answer, at the feet of

Notre Dame des Victoires in Paris. " When I took Holy Orders ten years ago," he wrote to Mère Marie-Eugénie, " I was as a blind man, in the sense that I could not see clearly the road I must walk. Today, my star has reappeared, and I believe I have discovered an objective towards which to direct my steps." With his eyes raised to that new star of decision, he came in June or July, 1845, to the feet of Our Lady, and there pronounced his private vows of religion, writing them down that they might be fixed and final. The great step had been taken, and the way was open, in the Providence of God, to the fulfilment of a great design. This fulfilment called for followers, and the magnetism of Father d'Alzon soon drew a small group of men who showed for a while the zeal of first fine rapture, but who were not destined to be the real beginning of his work.

" On December 25th, 1845," writes Father Vailhé (*Vie :* vol. I p. 394), " the Founder began with five companions ; on December 25th, 1850, he pronounced his first (public) vows with four disciples—and not one of those was there five years previously." What of this five-year interim ? Father Vailhé says one is tempted to call it a period of " stagnation "—and Father d'Alzon himself, feeling that he was thwarted at every hand must have felt it like that too. What a tremendous harrowing of his soul it must all have been : the persistent refusal of the Bishop to take one step forward ; illness and lack of men and of money ; political disorders ; defections and domestic crises.

It argues a tremendously clear sense of vocation in Father d'Alzon that he refused to be daunted by it all, but continued with that magnificent tenacity of his along the way he had chosen, content to have " his own hands only for his servants," as he said, to sweep his room and make his bed, to move through the College at night in that white Augustinian habit which the Ladies of the Assumption had made for him, and which seemed to symbolize his conviction that his family would be born yet in strength. The strength to succeed was in the humility that knew how to stoop to the menial tasks that sanctify the souls of Religious, and how to show the way to his followers by taking the lowest place—this place being, at one time, a windowless room in an airless corner of the College.

The most painful aspect of all this for Father d'Alzon was the irresolution and opposition he met with from his Bishop. He endured all in silence for a time, but finally decided to clear up the whole matter fully with his Bishop. Two days later, he wrote to Mère Marie-Eugénie de Jesus :

"I asked him what he really and truly thought of the work. He answered that he wished me to commit all my ideas to writing and give them to him. I questioned him about the vows, and he said he did not wish me to deprive him of his priests without his permission. I told him that I was ready to give them to him, but this seemed to stun him somewhat. I asked him whether it was true that he had said he would ruin me. He vigorously and emphatically assured me that such a thought had never entered his mind, nor had he ever said anything of the sort. Finally, it was agreed that he would give me freedom of action but without authorizing me. He asked for a report of what I intended to do. I had all my work cut out for me, to avoid saying too much or too little . . "

It was certainly not a very encouraging kind of permission, this unauthorizing authorization, this pinched assent. But it was sufficient, and the reward of Father d'Alzon's determination was those words of Pope Pius IX, in 1847, when the double privilege of the Roman breviary and calendar was conferred on the Congregation of the Priests of the Assumption : "I know this worthy priest and it is with all my heart that I grant him this privilege. Tell him that he will always find me ready to second his pious desires and good works. Let him ask and he will receive."

It is not within the scope of this book to follow Father d'Alzon any further in the fascinating story of the Fathers of the Assumption. This story is a book in its own right, and in attempting to confine it to the limits of a chapter, one is conscious all the time of the magnificent detail that is being crowded into a sentence, or crowded out altogether because of one's limits. We must glance, however, at some of those men who came forward to stand with Father d'Alzon as the heroic "masons" of his great work. "If God is the architect," he had written to his Bishop, "the masons will come forward later. Let me do my job of work in digging the foundations . . ."

The masons did come forward. There was Etienne Pernet, destined to make a glorious addition to the Assumptionist family by founding the " Little Sisters of the Assumption," and whose story I have told in "The Swallows of the Garret ". There was Victor Cardenne, who had lived a Bohemian life in Paris, gay and Godless, till the death of a loved one brought him up sharply, and he made his way back to the Church along the way of privation and suffering. In the *Croquis*, we meet him as a man who could combine deep religious virtues with a delicious sense of the comic, and knew how to employ his art of buffoonery in leading boys to laugh their way, as it were, along the road of virtue. He is the most colourful figure of the group, and in some ways the most human. " Cardenne had a genius for the comic," writes Canon Galeran. " The old pupils of the Assumption have said that they never met his like. They also said that by means of his comic roles, this incomparable master exercised a real apostolate among his pupils . . ." There was Henri Brun, in many ways the very antithesis in disposition of Victor Cardenne : the kind of man whose solid four-square qualities, whose caution and prudence, are of such importance to any nascent institution.

And finally, there was Hippolyte Saugrain whom we isolate here for special attention because he was to figure so much in what is our main concern here : the Oblates of the Assumption. Hippolyte first came into contact with the fiery enthusiasm of Father d'Alzon in 1846, when the latter was preaching a course of Lenten sermons in Notre Dame des Victoires, Paris. " Father d'Alzon was more than once under the impression ", writes Father Polyeucte Guissard (*Portraits Assomptionistes* p. 4) " that he had cast out his net to gather in a miraculous draught of fishes, that he would find among the young men of his audience his first group of disciples. But the desires and resolutions he had awakened did not outlive the day, because they were simply fires of straw ". However, there was one who came once only, but who carried away a spark that did not sink into the ashes of dead desires, and who travelled, early in August, 1846, to offer himself to Father d'Alzon in Nîmes. This was Hippolyte Saugrain, " a robust *Normand*, square-shouldered and sober-minded ". He did not come trailing clouds of academic glory; for he had made several attempts to master the rudiments of Latin and had failed. Then his parents had sent him to work in a drapery shop in Paris, where the liberty, libertinism and religious indifference of his associates led him astray for a time. When he shook himself free of this, the desire for the priesthood came alive in him again, and once more he laid siege to the mysteries of the Latin grammar. But the way of learning was steep for him almost to the extent of being vertical, and it was only his own splendid tenacity and dogged devotion to the resolution he had taken, that enabled him to climb twelve arduous years to his ordination at the age of thirty-six. " I am in your hands," he said to Father d'Alzon. " Make of me, I do not say what you *wish*, but at least what you *can*." It was the fitting reward of such humility that, at a time when Father d'Alzon was afflicted with a malady that lasted four years, it was this very Hippolyte, this poor grinder at grammar, who carried the whole burden of the College, and who had the reward of all those anxious years when he saw his great Founder rise to his feet to offer a toast : " I drink to the man who saved the Assumption." Another glory in the Assumptionist crown of Father Hippolyte, as we shall see, was that he played a magnificent part in the foundation of the Oblates of the Assumption, the final work with which Father d'Alzon completed the realization of his Assumptionist ideal.

To set the scene for the completion of that ideal, we must now turn our thoughts to the schism-torn East, to which, as we shall see, Father d'Alzon's thoughts were providentially directed, and which prepared the way for the coming of the Oblates.

THE CROWN OF THE IDEAL

About the year 1860, there was a strong current of feeling among the Bulgarians of the Turkish Empire in favour of political and religious independence. Since 1453, Christians were tended by bishops appointed by the Greek Orthodox Church, and these prelates were remarkable for their venality and corruption. In pursuance of their aims, some of the Bulgarian leaders were in favour of reunion with Rome, and when this resulted in an act of union (Constantinople, 24th December, 1860), the Sublime Porte gave his approval because he saw in it a means of withdrawing the Bulgarians from Russian influence. It is already clear how many twisted strands of politics have begun to weave themselves into the religious picture. There were the astute Bulgarian leaders, holding in their hands the trump card of union with Rome ; the Sublime Porte stood smilingly by ; and Russia watched to make the next move, which she did by proposing the establishment of a Bulgarian patriarchate independent of Rome and Constantinople. On January 21st, 1861, the new Bishop, Mgr. Sokolski, had been appointed, and Pope Pius IX consecrated him in Rome the following April. He was promptly kidnapped, taken to Russia, and confined to a monastery in Kiev until his death.

These few details are necessary to explain why, when Father d'Alzon arrived in Rome with his Bishop and a group of Nîmes pilgrims for the Canonization of the martyrs of Japan, the thought of Bulgaria should have been so much to the fore in the thoughts of Pius IX. At the public audience on June 5th, a remarkable thing happened : the Pope turned to Father d'Alzon and blessed his works " in the East and in the West." D'Alzon was indeed bewildered, for he had no works in the East ; but he was not left long without enlightenment. The following day, the Pope received him in private audience, and two months later, Father d'Alzon spoke publicly of its outcome : " I came away with the right—I might almost say the *mission*—to study the question of the return of those oriental peoples to the faith, and, with the help of some eminent persons, to seek out the means which must be adopted to achieve this aim indicated to me . . ." With characteristic enthusiasm he set about realizing these means, and at the Fifth General Chapter of the Fathers of the Assumption (Nîmes, September, 1862). Father Victorin Galabert was appointed as Founder of the Assumption Mission in the East.

Father Galabert resembled Father d'Alzon in many ways ; he, too, had that strong, vigorous, enterprising character needed in a pioneer. He had qualified brilliantly as a doctor of medicine in Montpellier, and had then turned aside from the splendid career assured to him, in order to devote himself to the Assumptionist ideal as a disciple of Father d'Alzon. His studies in Rome made him eminent as a theologian and a canonist—but more important than all that was his magnificent development in the religious life. Like Father d'Alzon, he was an ascetic ; he invariably retired to rest about eleven at night, and rose at three next morning, to work steadily through a day where his only nourishment was a meal taken about half-past twelve. His spiritual life was characterized by an intense devotion to the Blessed Eucharist, and this, as we shall see, was of immense significance in one appointed to be the inspiration of a spiritual renaissance in the East. He was thirty two years old at the time of his appointment, and was destined to make a tremendous impression on the Eastern people—an impression which was echoed in many testimonies paid to him in Rome at the time of the Vatican Council.

On February 14th, 1863, Father d'Alzon himself embarked at Marseilles, his destination being Constantinople. One wonders whether at this moment he recalled those words of his former Bishop saying that every Founder is a madman ; at all events, he seems to have been at once invigorated and stunned by the sheer audacity of the whole undertaking, for at that very moment he wrote a short note to one of his penitents : " What an adventure ! But I suppose we must be mad for Our Lord's sake ! . ." That streak of what we might call his divinely inspired insanity has come down undiminished through his years. There is no dust on the enthusiasm with which he takes his place on that boat ; it is the same fiery spirit rising to meet another impossible task. There are seventeen years of life left to him, and another splendid work to be done. As yet, he does not see clearly the shape of that work. He will see the need for it in the East, and he will return to Nîmes to pour all the riches of his intense living, of his deep spiritual worth, into the soul of the woman through which this—the crown of his work, the last stones of the Assumptionist house—is to be realized. Meantime, we follow him to the East.

Arrived in Constantinople, he set to work with that intense energy which seemed as necessary to him as the air he breathed. *Ubi d'Alzon ibi plenitudo actionis*, might be inscribed over every moment of his career. His Lenten preaching drew crowds, and every Catholic institution in the town felt his coming like a vigorous breeze, for he visited them all. But he was there principally to study the question of reunion with Rome, and it did not take long for that keen intelligence of his to pierce to the hollow heart of it all. A letter to Mère Eugénie contains these significant words : " Between you and me, this Bulgarian business is just fizzling out. There is more of politics than of religion in their dispositions towards Reunion . . . but I am far from wishing to give them up." Those last words are full of fine courage, for there was much else to blacken the picture of spiritual life in the East. He suffered intensely from the sight of the disrespect shown to the Blessed Eucharist, and his years were to be henceforward filled with his cry to his future spiritual daughters to make reparation :

" Ah ! . . . what reparation must we not make to Our Lord for the injuries which He receives in these countries ! Just think—they consecrate viaticum for the sick on Holy Thursday only, and it is left in damp places, so that after a certain time, it is simply a sodden infected mass. Is Jesus Christ present ? Is He not ? Who can say ! If He is, what profanation ! If He is no longer present, what do the sick receive ? Since they communicate under both species, and the Precious Blood cannot be conserved ; since, moreover, and thank God for it—it never enters the heads of these priests to say Mass with any frequency, this is how they act when they are called on to minister to anyone. They take a little of this dried up or musty bread, dip it in a glass of wine and give it to the dying person. It is with this viaticum that their baptized souls appear before God. Does not all this make us shiver with horror ! . . ."

Such was his impression of the Orthodox clergy, against whom, indeed, Father Galabert warns him, for, in the short time he was already there, this founder of the Assumptionist Mission had come to realize what reserve was necessary in dealing with a vocationless, greed-ridden, slothful and spineless clergy. That the people themselves were good, served only to throw all this into relief. " The Bulgarian people are good, but not their leaders, either religious or political," is Father d'Alzon's summary of the situation. He read no discouragement into all this ; for this man, who said he had adopted his motto *Adveniat Regnum Tuum*, " almost by instinct ", found the words of that motto clamorously about him in such just situations. It was against difficulties and acute disappointments that Father d'Alzon began his effective work in the East. It is outside our scope to trace this in detail, as we must hasten on to study in all its humble splendour, the work to whch, undoubtedly, in the last phase of his life, he gave his heart and all the best that was in him. Here, again, the first stage was filled with disappointment, simply because, in the designs of God, this final work of his crowded life was to be one pre-eminently his own.

From the moment he received what he called his " mission " from Pope Pius IX, Father d'Alzon realized that he must have missionary nuns as the priest's right hand on the mission field. Naturally, he turned to Mère Eugénie on his return to Nîmes, for he held a unique position both as her spiritual director and as the spiritual mainstay of her work. How greatly Mère Eugénie figured in the life of Father d'Alzon, and he in her life, is evinced by the immense correspondence between them—in which, incidentally, the number of his letters is far greater than that of his spiritual daughter's replies to him. The outcome of his appeal to her for help on the Missions was that, after having raised his hopes even to the extent of his writing to Father

Galabert to announce their coming, she eventually decided against it entirely. Such a summary dismissal of the matter may give a wrong impression of that great spiritual genius, Mère Eugénie, and we are far from intending to do that. Her reluctance to accede to Father d'Alzon's request was due to a certain fear of a new branch—though indeed a branch which was originally envisaged in the foundaton of the Nuns of the Assumption, a branch of *Oblates* between the *Choir Sisters* and the *Lay-Sisters*—being grafted on her Congregation. There was also, it would seem the question of a lack of personnel. The story of the *Oblates* as eventually founded by Father d'Alzon, contains plenty of evidence to show the benevolence and charity of Mère Eugénie and her daughters towards the new foundation. At the time, however, her refusal was a disappointment to Father d'Alzon. He was, as he himself put it, " up against a brick wall." And it is characteristic of a man like him that he does not stay looking dejectedly at the wall, but turns about and looks elsewhere. This is precisely what he did.

He appealed to the Dominican Sisters, to the Sisters of Charity of Besançon, to the Francisan Nuns—but all of these had their hands too full already. What next ? There remained only God to whom he could turn, and—we say it for him—there was, of course, d'Alzon himself. How many times in his life had he been obliged to turn from others when he was faced with the seemingly impossible, and do it himself. Very well, I'll do it myself ! D'Alzon never said these words explicitly, but his whole life said them for him. So, once again, and in the final glorious gesture of his life, he turned round and . . . founded another Congregation !

In 1864, we find that he has selected as the corner-stone of his new foundation, a certain Mlle Pauline—a refined, educated and determined person. Here we meet Marie, Father d'Alzon's sister, in the picture for a moment, when as Madame de Puységur and mistress of the fine property of Lavagnac, she took a lively and practical interest in the formation of Mlle Pauline. Father d'Alzon devoted himself to her spiritual training, and to the gathering together of the first group of his Oblates. He arranged for her to enter for a while among the Nuns of the Assumption, and then wrote with joyful anticipation : " The group of Oblates is being organized. The foundation stone—Pauline—is in Retreat. Next week we shall have two more, then, two others . . ." But next week brought its cruel disappointment. News came that Pauline had changed her mind, and had asked to join the Ladies of the Assumption. Again, it was " the brick wall " for Father d'Alzon—again the sense of frustration, for he had certainly no one among the others capable of being invited to take her place. " No, I am not angry . . .", he writes. " It is a disappointment for me, which I shall add to other disappointments, and which serves to detach from the world and impel towards God . . . One thing, however, was abundantly clear : he was far from beaten.

When Father d'Alzon met with this disappointment in his choice of Pauline as the person whose name would be entered in that blank space he had left at the head of the list of Oblates, he thought to choose from among his group of pious ladies in Nîmes a very fervent soul called Mlle Eulalie de Régis. But there was a greater call on the charity of Mlle Eulalie : she had to devote her life to the care of her sick father. Moreover, her own health was very poor. She longed to follow the desire of her heart and become an Oblate, and being unable to do so, she devoted herself to the utmost of her power to forwarding and fostering the great work. Father d'Alzon paid fitting tribute to her in a fine letter to his Oblates. " Although ", he writes " she was not the first with whom the idea of your foundation was discussed, there was nothing to equal the manner in which she devoted herself, with all the energy of her vigorous nature, to the ideal of preparing missionary nuns for the East and for countries where workers were needed to proclaim the tidings of the Gospel. In this way, her love for Our Lord found a means of reaching out to the uttermost parts of the earth. Her last and most lively yearnings were for you . . . Your progress, your sanctification were ceaselessly in her thoughts, and it can be said that, when she departed from you, no one was a greater Oblate at heart than she." Father d'Alzon regarded Eulalie de Régis as a great spiritual power in the first years of the Oblates—a power that lived after her. " I am convinced", he

he knew his limitations very well, and behind the voice of Father d'Alzon pleading for a Sister from Mère Eugénie, we constantly hear the voice of Father Hippolyte. It was a great joy to him when, late in July, the longed-for Sister arrived, and that joy increased a hundred-fold when it became more and more evident how wisely and how well the foundress had chosen when she sent Mère Marie Madeleine to guide the first Oblates. She was recalled by her Superior in 1867, and her two years left a deep impression on the infant group.

There is a tribute paid by one of her own Sisters to Mère Marie Madeleine which is of great significance for the position she was now called upon to fill. " Mère Marie Madeleine does everything in such a charitable way. What a virtuous and courageous soul in all circumstances ; what self-forgetfulness without a shadow of self-love." Heavy burdens of responsibility were placed upon her, and the cross of physical suffering constantly shadowed her. In the last three years of her life she walked with her God in darkness—for she had gradually lost her sight. Her death was a very painful one, but marked with that strength and heroism which she had once given so generously to the first Oblates. Her name was held in great reverence by them. When she was recalled from Le Vigan, her place was taken by Mère Emmanuel d'Everlange, who continued to guide the Oblates until the coming of her who was chosen to be their Mother.

For there was a blank space in that list of six drawn up by Father d'Alzon. The names were numbered—but the numbers began with 2. After the number 1 the space was blank, and the name had yet to be inserted at the head of the book that tells the Oblates' story. Father d'Alzon had been disappointed in his first two attempts to fill this gap. " What is most remarkable in your very humble yet very powerful origins," he wrote in the letter we have quoted above, " is that everything turned out contrary to all our expectations." That name was to be that of Marie Correnson (Mère Emmanuel Marie de la Compassion) whom Father d'Alzon had chosen as Foundress. She has perhaps the unique distinction of being a Foundress who comes to her Congregation some years after it was founded. How that was so is the external story of Marie Correnson.   But there is a much more wonderful story to be told of how a spiritual giant reached out inspired hands to her, and lifted her soul to the heroic heights of a mighty ideal.

THE MOTHER FOUNDRESS

The prelude to the birth of Marie Correnson, destined in the designs of God to be Father d'Alzon's great instrument in found-ing his *Oblates*, was one of those appalling train crashes which, in the early days of railways, were all the more gruesome because the coaches were locked. On May 8th, 1842, the axle of the Paris-Versailles train snapped, and the train was derailed; the coaches crashed into one another and were concertinaed; fire broke out. The coaches, being of light construction, left little to hope for; the agonized cries of the trapped victims filled the air and there were many deaths. Somewhere in the torn wreckage a man had succeeded, after many efforts, in getting out. Boiling water from the broken pipes scorched his feet badly as he helped his wife through the passage to safety. She was thoroughly shaken, and on her return to Paris, she fell seriously ill. She was carrying her first child at the time and it was feared that perhaps the accident would prove fatal to the birth of the child. However, on July 20th, the child was born, but the accident had left its mark. The little girl was destined to be always physically small and frail. Such then, was the birth of Marie, eldest daughter of Doctor and Madame Correnson. But nature makes its compensations, and sometimes a frail body houses a delicate and very lively spirit. This was the case with Marie. Under the guidance of tutors specially chosen for her, she made rapid progress in her studies, and quickly gave proof of the sensitive mind with which she was endowed.

Doctor Correnson was Doctor to the College of the Assump-tion in Nîmes, and was an intimate friend of Father d'Alzon. The llitte Marie often met Father d'Alzon as a visitor to her home, and as she grew older, she began to be attracted towards him because she was sensitive to the virile spirituality that went out from him. The Correnson home was a deeply Catholic one. When the time came for Marie and her younger sister,

Augustine, to make their First Communion, Madame Correnson confided them to the care of the Nuns of the Visitation at Avignon, in order that their preparations might be as perfect as possible. This early taste of the religious atmosphere of the Convent was destined to have a shaping effect on the life-design of each of these girls. Father d'Alzon, as the years went on, realized more and more the sterling qualities that were latent in them, to be developed by instruction and by a deepening of their character through prayer. Marie, in particular, chose him for her spiritual guide. She was intelligent enough to know that this guidance would be accepted as a positive task by Father d'Alzon, and that he would really be her guide ; what she could not have guessed, however, was that in choosing him she had chosen the power that was to shape the pattern of all her years. For the moment, all she knew was that this priest was taking a deep, personal, sympathetic interest in her spiritual progress, as though that progress was something vital to him ; and that he was directing her assiduously into works of charity and of apostolic zeal. For his own part, he saw that perhaps some day she would become a Nun of the Assumption—a daughter of Mère Marie Eug´nie, and he was directing her with a view to this ; for as yet he was not aware that there was something providential to the working out of the design of his own life, in this intense interest he was taking in Marie Correnson.

The idea that she might indeed be the person to take that Number One place he had left vacant, seems to have come to him gradually. He began by speaking to her about the preparation she must make " for the activity God may ask." Though still not thinking of her as a possible *Oblate*, he calls on her to be the protectress of the Oblates. When the first glimmerings of the idea came to him, it was accompanied by hesitation on his part : " *As to becoming an Oblate yourself, that is another question. I would only wish it, if there were several of you (of the same social standing and education) to join that little family in order to do it good and to derive good from it . . .*" But eight days after this was written, he came to a clear decision, and invited her to join him in his new work : " *Do you feel you have the courage to enter, by easy stages, more fully into the work ?* " he asks her. " *While remaining outside for a while, do you think you could become, one day, its Mother? Would you have enough patience to endure criticism . . . ? . . . certain unpleasant people . . . ?*" So question followed question in this decisive letter, each question designed to help Marie to search into herself for that singleness of spiritual vision which would enable her to rise above all considerations of gentility and class, to the supernatural disinterestedness he was asking from her. Now, Marie had been one of the ladies from Nîmes who had assisted at the first clothing of the Oblates, and on her own admission she had shed some tears of disappointment that Father d'Alzon had not asked her to be of their number. She had been kept in touch with all that was going on, and had helped in many ways. Yet now, when she was asked, she found that the social barrier between her and those daughters of the mountains who were the first Oblates, made her pause, and she wrote to Father d'Alzon to say so. We shall meet his reply when we deal with the spiritual formation of Marie Correnson, in the second part of this chapter. It is sufficient to note that he met Marie's social hesitation with the shattering reply that pointed to a God made man. What, Marie—he said in effect—did not God stoop a great deal lower than you are being asked to do? . . . It was only a very human moment of final hesitation, understandable in one so bred to " class " as Marie must certainly have been. That moment disappeared forever when Marie read, with feelings of deep remorse, that reply from Father d'Alzon, and her life's aim henceforth was to become the living image of his ideal of an Oblate, that she might stamp that image on many souls.

There was strong and sustained opposition to her decision from her family, and therefore Father d'Alzon decided that she had better receive the veil secretly. The ceremony took place on Passion Sunday, 1867, in the Chapel of the Assumption, Nîmes. She was dispensed from wearing the veil till she officially entered the convent. The document attesting the clothing was drawn up by Father d'Alzon, and signed by him, by Marie, and by the seven Oblate Sisters who were present. She received the name Emmanuel-Marie de la Compassion—a name, as her spiritual Father was to point out so often to her, signifying suffering and the deep understanding born of suffering. Like Mary, she was to bring forth her spiritual children in suffering ; she was to learn what it means to be a spiritual Mother.

It was absolutely impossible for Marie to live in her family circle without the discovery being made that her heart was elsewhere. Her parents made it as difficult as possible for her, with the result that her time of waiting for a definite call from Father d'Alzon, must have been extremely painful. Finally, on what Father d'Alzon was later to call " that famous June 27 " (1868), Marie, after a year's noviciate, left her home after Mass without saying good-bye to her parents. We gather something of the family reaction from a letter of Father d'Alzon's (June 27th. 1868) :

My very dear child,

You can imagine how my heart has been with you the whole day. Augustine will give you a full account of what has happened. Your father said his say—but really very little ; he said that his daughter had no heart . . . Your mother is worried because you have gone without your hat. Augustine did not tell her that you no longer needed it . . . Your grandfather, M. Pleindoux, went to see your mother, and they wept together. Your father was silent at dinner. Your mother and your grandfather ate nothing at all . . . Your grandfather summed all up by saying : " We are returning to the Middle Ages . . . "

The grandfather was the most violent in his reactions ; when speaking with Father Galabert on a journey from Alais to Nîmes, he listened in silence to some remarks about the Oblates, but then blurted out that in his opinion Father d'Alzon was both stupid and crazy. (Father d'Alzon's letter : 23rd August, 1867). Marie had made her big decision and had taken the great step on the verge of which she had at first hesitated. That this step should have been an occasion for sorrow and bitter words among those most dear to her, must have caused her acute suffering. But she had made her decision foreseeing all that, and knowing that the decision God sometimes asks of a soul is as a sword that pierces the human heart of a family. A bigger family awaited her at Le Vigan—that family of simple souls who had the courage to step into the unknown that they might become the foundation of a great venture for God. They were a family without a mother; but now that Mother had come to them, anxious to bring them a mother's heart.

Such is the story of the external life of Marie Correnson, and it is another wonderful example of how God weaves the pattern of His designs; but yet more wonderful is the weaving of the invisible pattern—the pattern of the spirituality of Marie Correnson.

It is fascinating to watch the sensitive hands of the potter on his clay; and the image suggests itself when one reads the magnificent letters of Father d'Alzon to his spiritual daughter. In them we see him moulding and shaping her soul to the great work for which he had chosen her. Through those letters, we are as it were made spectators of Marie Correnson's spiritual growth to the full maturity of a Foundress. He selects her deliberately for his great work, and he puts before her an exact and exacting ideal towards which she is to strive with all that is in her. " Above all, I ask for you that strong life of sacrifice and of immolation, such as should be that of a true Christian in our days when we are witnessing such impoverishment of character, and such laxity of conduct all around us."

Very soon, Marie felt that strong spiritual hands were being laid on her, urging her forward, never giving her much time to sink back into the comfort of a mediocre spirituality. " *You are much in my thoughts, my dear Marie; especially do I think of you in the presence of Our Lord. I ask of Him that your whole life should be His, and that, since you wish to separate yourself from the world, you may learn in the midst of the world to make for yourself a Solitude in Him and find your apostolate in Him.*" Thus, in those years when, as we have seen, he thought it best that she should remain in her home, he laboured to penetrate her soul with that silence, that solitude, in which alone the seeds of spiritual greatness can germinate. Though she is in the world, he calls on her to be " *the heart of the work . . . by giving your life to it through hidden action, through holy desires, through prayer and immolation, through your efforts to lay at the Saviour's feet all the sweet perfumes of your soul, and thus to obtain all the light, the strength and the help of which an apostolic family is in need. Hence my dear daughter, you are entrusted with a mission ; you are appointed to be the provider of the spiritual graces of the Assumption.*" This was the formulation of her secret mission, which was designed to be the driving force, the unifying central idea of all her spirituality. "*Ask also of God that He may send great and holy defenders to His Church, like those who now rest in the tomb before the end of the combats.*" He would have her, therefore, to live deeply within herself, laying her own spiritual foundation deep and firm ; but always with her eyes raised to the meaning of it all—to the great mission before her, to that shining citadel that was all in all to Father d'Alzon : the Church. "*Would you like to help me to found a work whose aim would be to make reparation for the insults offered to Our Saviour in the Blessed Sacrament in the East, and to foster His cult and His love ? The great devotion of our times, in face of Protestant denials, must be the exaltation of the Church, the cult of the Blessed Virgin and love for the Holy Eucharist . . .*"

There is a terrific urgency about his appeals to her, as though he has really given his heart to this his final " dream " and has become convinced, with a calm and strong certainty, that on Marie his work is to be founded. "*The Christian life*" he says to her, "*takes on very beautiful proportions today for those who are willing to accept it with its severe labours, its struggles, its flung horizons. One must needs have an alert eye and a calm head to plunge into the abysses which are opening. I do not know why I dream that my dear Marie must contemplate all that is happening, so that from it she may learn how to achieve a true beauty, of purity, of greatness and of devotion. This is my dream. Make my dream a reality . . .*" Like the king's daughter, he would have her beauty to be " within." He demands from her nothing less than that she should strive *to become perfect. " There are different degrees of perfection. I demand from you all that God expects from you. Understand me well : none other than all that—yes, and with no exception. I have emphasised a thousand times to you : let there be nothing extraordinary about your external conduct, but all delicacy of heart, all enthusiasm, all prudence, tact, and courage to confess Christ usefully, apostolically, so that you can say of yourself : ' I no longer belong to myself, but am become in the hands of my Spouse an instrument from whose strings He can draw the*

FATHER D'ALZON IN HIS MATURITY

music that hymns His mercy and His love.' Be a saint ; *begin your work !* " Perfection, he points out to her, lies in the entire giving of self to God ; and he tells her magnificently what all this entails :

" *This greater giving of yourself to Our Lord must have a triple character of perseverance, of seriousness and of intimacy : of perseverance, that you may conquer the heights and the depths of your nature ; of seriousness, because in proportion as the soul plunges itself in the supernatural life, it develops an attitude of respect, of holy fear and wonder, which naturally makes it serious ; finally of intimacy, since it is a life lost in the love of Christ which is demanded of the soul. Your furrow is fully marked for you, and I indeed hope that you will deviate neither to the right or to the left.*"

There is ample evidence that he aimed *consciously* at stamping her spirituality with his own ideas—that he wished those ideas to be incarnated in his *Oblates*, and therefore, supremely, in her whom he had chosen to be their Mother. " *I would have you to be my true daughter. I know you are so in your heart ; but I wish you to become so too by a body of ideas which I want you to make entirely yours . . . Tomorrow I shall be fifty years old. I am not young any more, and God alone knows how many years remain to me. If it be his will, I am very anxious to leave behind me a series of ideas which I think will help the development of the Kingdom of Christ. Perhaps it is stupid pride that makes me say that ; but it is very true that I see clearly a great work to be done. My daughter, I want you to be able to help me to do that work . . .*" He asks her to co-operate through sacrifice and prayer ; indeed, through all the letters runs the constant refrain : " *Become a child of prayer, and in prayer, a child of sacrifice.*"

There is a splendid tone of spiritual intimacy in these letters ; and once he revealed to her the innermost recesses of his heart, in which we are given a precious glimpse into the interior of his own soul, and the dynamic thoughts that live there are as the spring of his inspiration :

" *I want to be a man of faith, of prayer, of true humility ; a religious penetrated with the spirit of sacrifice ; serious, in the true sense of the word ; above all, a religious whose least action, whose words and conduct*

*are supernatural ; a superior preoccupied with the duty of developing and
of sanctifying his spiritual family in charity, union, love of our Lord,
of the Blessed Virgin, of the Church, according to the perfection of the
evangelical counsels and of apostolic zeal. But indeed, my daughter, I
am nothing of all that ! When I think of what we could do, if we had
a little zeal for the cause of God, I am indeed dismayed. Sometimes
I dream . . . and I lose myself in aspirations which will never be
realized.*"

When a man flings so widely and so generously the horizons
of his desire to further the Kingdom of God, and when he brings
to it the energy of an Emmanuel d'Alzon, we view his achievements with astonishment. But a passage like this leads us
behind those achievements into the very heart of the man, and
shows us that divine discontent in him reaching its hands towards
the impossible. Emmanuel d'Alzon worked like ten men, and
chafed inwardly all the time because the visions of his desires
were beyond the capacity of those ten men in him. It is a passage
like that which shows us the secret of all he achieved.

" *God first gives Himself ; but when the soul gives itself in its turn,
there is then a reciprocity which in some way makes it necessary for God
to be the conqueror in all things, above all in generosity ; and it is impossible to say what new bounties, what fresh tenderness He will invent
provided He finds in the soul love and sacrifice.*"

It is thus that he constantly appeals to her, inviting her to
measure her generosity with that of God, confident that she will
be vanquished. " *This is a great and solemn thing for you . . . and
I speak in all sincerity when I say that I am profoundly moved when I
think that I am mapping the course of the future life of a child who is so
deeply loved, and to whom, nevertheless, I am holding out only a crown of
thorns and the nails of the Cross.*"

All this spiritual preparation was going on secretly side by
side in Father d'Alzon's mind, with the actual foundation of the
Oblates. But at the last moment, Marie shrank from his call,
because she felt the delicacy of her birth and upbringing. One
can imagine what a blow this must have been for Father d'Alzon,
and yet one feels that the strange firm conviction he had about
her did no more than flicker for a moment of disappointment.

His reply to her is splendidly restrained, and shows how calm such a reputedly impetuous man could be in his real moments of crisis :

" *My very dear Child,*

Your letter does not surprise me ; I even admit that I was somewhat expecting it. But I think that your present repugnances will be for you one day, a subject of very deep humiliation when, in seeking to walk in the footsteps of Our Lord, you will consider that after all, in order to unite Himself with humanity, Our Lord has covered a little more ground in descending from heaven to sinners, than you would do in stepping from your position to that of my poor children. Do you know, my dear Marie, I blame myself for your discouragement ? If I had only preached to you by example the true apostolic life, you would have understood a little better the beauty of this life ; for when Christ planned the apostolic life, He began by first choosing fishermen, and men of common clay, and we have begun with our mountain daughters. All this I assure you, is very simple in my eyes, and I thank you for having spoken to me with admirable frankness. Attached to you as I am, I would be merely hoodwinking myself were I to say that this has not made me suffer. But look you, Marie, there is One whom I love a thousand times more than I love you, and that One is Christ ; and I can find no better occasion of offering to Him a very inadequate reparation for all the injuries I have done Him, than by accepting . . . the news that I am to be alone where I thought that you and I would stand together. I am a little embarrassed ; I fear that what I have said may annoy you, and yet, the voice of friendship tells me that I ought to reveal to you all the recesses of my soul. What is true friendship, if not that ? You are not yet perfect I know, but you want to become so. I know no better way for you to do so than that which I have shown you. If I am wrong, tell me so . . ."

Such a letter, so full of gentle rebuke and gentle sorrow, could not fail to go straight to the heart of this generous girl whose hesitation in taking the step out of the social sphere to which she had been bred, was very natural indeed. But the manner in which he so gently put such hesitation side by side with the abysmal humiliation of her God (*He emptied Himself*, St. Paul has said), swept away the indecision and made her blush deeply for it. Perhaps, too, she remembered that the man who spoke to her in this letter was the same who had turned away from turreted Lavagnac and had chosen the rue de l'Arc du Gras! One can well imagine with what feelings of self-reproach Marie read that postscript to the letter : " *On re-reading this, I find that perhaps I have phrased it a little warmly. But I know well what I am saying, and I am sure that you will read with understanding . . .*" With this letter, Marie was won again to a cause from which she had wavered in a human moment. From henceforth, she was to devote herself to realising in herself the ideas of a great man who knew how to point out to her the best way. D'Alzon was not to stand alone ; for she had been ignited with the fire of his zeal, and it was to burn brightly in her to the very end.

From this point onwards, Father d'Alzon's direction and formation of Marie Correnson becomes more intense and more directed towards her mission of forming in others " the dream he had dreamed in his heart." " *My conviction grows deeper and deeper every day that God is giving you a very painful, very difficult, very delicate and very beautiful mission . . . I scarcely seem to wish for any other subject in my conversation in prayer with Christ than that of oyur mission.*" The spirit she must cultivate in preparation for that mission must be characterised above all by apostolic zeal. " *The virtue which must dominate all the others in your soul is apostolic zeal.*" This virtue must manifest itself by a great expansion of heart, a blossoming, a flinging open of the gates of goodwill, that God may enter and ask what he wills. " *I must not hide from you that the work which you undertake will be as great as the generosity of your heart allows . . .*" " *The Oblates are called to do all that the good God may ask of them. I am convinced that we stand in need of every quality to fulfil our mission.*" This emphasis on suppleness as fundamental to the spirit of the Oblates sank deep into the heart of Marie Correnson, and was expressed in those words which were to become the motto of their Congregation : *Ecce Ego, Mitte Me*—Here am I, send me : words which express that joyful willingness to undertake anything, which Father d'Alzon said should be a synonym for their spirit. But this was to be no mere " activism," but was to well up from a deep religious life, " per redundantiam a contemplatione "—as St. Thomas Aquinas had said. Hence the tremendous and reiterated

emphasis which Father d'Alzon puts on the interior life as the
source of all Marie's spiritual strength :

" *For your part, my child you must practise abundantly the Presence
of God. All your thoughts and fancies of whatever kind, must no
longer be otherwise than inducements to draw you to this Divine Presence.
Remember incessantly that it is under the eye of our Divine Master that
you must work ; it is into His Being that you must allow yourself to be
absorbed. You are His instrument, but an instrument which, one day
must cause many other instruments to vibrate in harmony with you. You
must be a mother, and it is in virtue of this title that you must draw
nearer to the Blessed Virgin. Be a mother to the little apostolic
family confided to you, as the Blessed Virgin was the mother of the
apostles before being their queen . . .*"

It is thus filled with the power that comes from living in the
presence of God that he would have her " infiltrate"—this is his own
word—his ideas to his daughters. It is a well known phenomen
that if a stringed instrument is plucked, the vibrations will
call forth an answering note from another instrument at the same
pitch although a hand has not touched it. He puts the analogy
before Marie here, to show her how directly he would have his
daughters respond to her spirit—and therefore how important
it was that she should be impregnated with Christ.

Within two days after the passage we have quoted, we find
him writing these lines to Marie, which must surely be among
his most lovely : " *But my dear child, let me point out to you that life
falls into two parts : what we do, and what we are. What you are
doing or what you ought to do, is what you now know very well. You
must do the work of an Oblate, as your sister (who is to enter the
Carmel) . . . hopes to do the work of a Carmelite. But what you
ought to be is something quite different. This is the other part of life—
a wholly interior life in the presence of God, lived in silence, adoration,
love. What you ought to be is achieved by an incessant struggle, by a
complete detachment from the world and from self, by a perpetual
sacrifice of your own will, by that eager flight of the arrow which seeks
its target, of the flame that climbs towards the sky, of the love that flies
towards God and suffers until it becomes one with Him. Oh ! dear
little mother, when will you be like that ? A true spouse, a veritable*

seraphim, ceaselessly consuming yourself until the moment when you are one with God! This is what I demand of you, and what I demand also of your sister Augustine . . . But indeed you are pledged to an even greater degree of love than is Augustine, because the flames of your love must be contagious flames which consume, not only your own soul, but all the spouses of Christ who are confided to you . . ."

This is indeed a splendid commentary on the idea that the greatest work of any soul is its own sanctification—the perfection of what it *is*, so that what it *does* may have spiritual worth. This perfect Marie, Father d'Alzon tells her, will be named Mère Emmanuel-Marie de la Compassion. "*My daughter, God will do great things with you if you learn to be His—to be a humble, supple, intelligent instrument in His hands. I wish that, on your way from Nîmes to Le Vigan, you could throw Marie Correnson out of the window of the stage coach, so that only Mère Emmanuel-Marie de la Compassion, clothed with the good garment of Christ, would arrive at Rochebelle!*" For he is sending her to his daughters that she may be the good odour of Christ to them. "*Yes, my poor little Mother, there are hard moments ahead of you. You have been well named Mère Emmanuel-Marie de la Compassion. I see in the trials before you, the promise of a rich harvest. Open wide your heart, fling wide your arms, and know that you stand in need of greater warmth and generosity than perhaps you realize, in order to take to your heart the family whose mother God wills that you should become. Stand on Calvary between the Blessed Virgin, your model, and Our Lord, your spouse. Ten months ago you had to suffer at Auteuil and at Ems. This year, you will suffer at Le Vigan; the following year it will be elsewhere, and so on to the end of your life.[1] It is very cruel of me thus to lead you to the cross. But I am convinced that you will thank me for it one day. Offer up some of your suffering for me, because I offer for your intention all that I can . . ."*

These last words are of great signifiance, for they complete the picture of the spiritual formation of Mère Emmanuel-Marie de la Compassion. He did not leave her alone to grope her way, but prayer for her was never far from his lips and his ardent desire for her sanctification was not less than for his own. "*But from Montpellier to Lavagnac, how often have I prayed the round of my beads for you? Thirty-six, my daughter—twelve complete rosaries,*

---

[1] This was somewhat in the nature of a prophecy. See Appendix One.

and I'm not sure that it was not thirteen . . ." Again : *" I have just said Mass not for you, but with you. You are seldom from my thoughts. If you could only know how I feel when I offer my daughters to Christ ! "* (Letter from Rome). *" I seem to desire scarcely any other subject of conversation with Christ than you and your spiritual welfare . . ."* And thus quotation could be heaped on quotation to show how Father d'Alzon was preoccupied with Marie Correnson as the vivifying centre of this, his last great work, the Oblates of the Assumption.

Deeply, passionately, he instilled his ideas into her ; and she in turn carried them alive into the souls of his Daughters. Thus was born the spirit of the Oblate Sisters of the Assumption. What that spirit was, and how it revealed itself in the splendid souls of those early years, must now occupy our attention.

LIVING EMBODIMENTS OF AN IDEAL

"*God, my child, will accomplish great things through you, if you are His humble, pliable, intelligent instrument*" . . . "*The Oblates are called to everything which the good God wishes from them*" . . . Thus Father d'Alzon to his Foundress.

In the heart of the mountains, where the little town of Le Vigan seems to hollow a place for itself among the grapes and the vines, young women had come together each with an ideal of selfless service in her heart. The beginnings were hard, and there was no hint of future softness or rest in the name "Bulgaria" which their Founder had given to their new home. Poverty and toil were the lot of each Oblate pioneer, and the most commodious part of their house seems to have been given over to the silk-worms, on which the Sisters eked out a bare existence. To-day, one leaves *La Condamine*—the birthplace of Father d'Alzon, now a convent of *Les Orantes*, the contemplatives of the Assumption—and by a winding way, past the grand old parish church where Father d'Alzon was baptized, one comes to the cradle of the Oblates. The house gives a curious impression of standing on stilts; the upper part, under the roof where there seems to be scarcely head-room, is where the Sisters lived and slept; below were the silk-worms' much more spacious and comfortable apartments. A ladder from the ground in the small courtyard ran up to a door in the upper part, and the ventilation was through curious egg-shaped windows, which must have been sometimes far from effective, and excessively inconvenient.

Here those first heroic souls laboured and prayed, tending the silk-worms, collecting the silk, their minds constantly lifted to the missionary ideal of self-effacement and selfless drudgery for Christ, which their Founder had given them. They were all very human too, as we see them, for example, in a letter Father d'Alzon wrote from Le Vigan in 1867 : "*The Oblates are doing very well. Yesterday it was found necessary to throw out an enormous quantity of silk. They were all in tears about it, except Sister Helen, who, having wept copiously in a similar situation some years ago, had resolved to remain dry-eyed and to say nothing. Nevertheless by the evening, all were very joyfully resigned to having worked so much to no purpose, because I asked them to offer up their disappointment to obtain for me a grace which I kept secret from them."* "*That grace,*" he goes on to tell Marie Correnson, "*was that you would not have too much difficulty to meet in coming to us*". Besides being a window opening on to these early years, this extract shows the spirit of simplicity reigning there, and the lovely childlike attitude towards their Founder. " It was terrible to have to throw out the work of all those months, and there were copious tears, but our Father wants us to offer it all up for his special intention, and so perhaps it is not all lost after all "—and the smiles returned.

We live in a sophisticated world where this may read as childish nonsense ; but probe it a little deeper, and you come upon the splendid, indomitable, selfless spirit that sent such souls, who had learned how to smile over lost endeavour, into the most unpromising regions of the mission field, where heroism was demanded of them as the stuff of their everyday life. There was a terrific concentration of spiritual effort and magnificent strivings to achieve personal holiness among these first Sisters, for the intrepid and fiery spirit of Emmanuel d'Alzon seemed to have entered into each and every one of them. The first fruits of it all were seen when, on April 25th, 1868, the pioneer group of five Oblates embarked at Marseilles, their destination being the ancient city of Constantinople in European Turkey, the first field of their apostolate.

It is a great moment in the life of every man of ideals when he can look on his dream and see it a reality. It must have been with a swelling *Te Deum* in his heart that Father d'Alzon stood on the quay on that April day, with his first five Oblates and their Mother. To complete his joy, Mère Eugénie de Jésus, that woman of delicate culture and spiritual genius, was also there to speak warm words of encouragement, to send her prayer after them over the water which rippled back in the wake of the ship, and to share humbly in this beginning of a new heroic venture. It is good to linger for a moment on this fine tableau, and see those great nineteenth-century figures standing side by side on the quay, as the last boat moves away and the white handkerchiefs flutter in farewell. The branches of the Assumption were united in that movement, and this decisive moment must have called down a blessing on them all. As Father d'Alzon and Mère Emmanuel-Marie turn away with their hearts full of prayerful exaltation, our thoughts go with that little band of five and we follow them over the water to where the heroism of pioneer tasks await their coming.

We know nothing about that sea journey, but we may guess at the great expectancy of the thoughts which filled each heart ; and if perhaps there was also a little loneliness, a little home-sickness for the mountains, lurking there, it must have been more than dispelled by the warm welcome given to them on their arrival at Constantinople by those magnificent doyennes of charity—the Sisters of Charity of St. Vincent de Paul. How often, in the history of new Foundations in the Church over the last two centuries, has not the name of these Sisters come up under similar conditions—arms flung wide in welcome when encouragement was most needed ! From there, the Oblates left by boat for Rhodosto, a little port on the Marmora. Here since life cannot always have compensations, they had to wait in vain for a representative of the French Consulate who never arrived.

Then one of those strange events occurred which sometimes erupt into the histories of sanctity, and which seem to transpose happenings from one plane to another with startling suddenness. The little group of five were waiting, probably at some dingy quay-side office ; time went on, hour followed hour, and the Sisters were hungry. Suddenly they saw a young man approach-ing them. He gave them a loaf of bread, and told them he had come to direct them to the French Consulate. Now, this is where the sudden change of plane occurs, for when he had taken them there, and they looked back for him, he had simply vanished into thin air. These five nuns were certainly not seers of non-existent wonders—no one could be of the school of Emmanuel d'Alzon and not have both spiritual feet planted firmly on the soil of commensense ; and yet, such was the impression this event made upon them, that they had no hesitation in believing that one of their Guardian Angels had taken this form in order to help them. The loaf must have been welcome, but of greater nourishment still must have been the spiritual uplift which came with the conviction that the hand offering the bread was perhaps that of an angel.

Their journey was indeed a thing of contrasts, for from this event of possibly an angelic nature, the Sisters turned to the very prosaic—painfully prosaic—joggings of an unsprung ox-waggon which took them over the last stage of their journey to Constantinople. From an account given by Father J. Davies, S.J., in the " Missionary Magazines of the Jesuit Mission ", (Vol. VI, No. 69) where the author describes a similar trek made by five intrepid Irish Dominican Sisters, we can reconstruct this journey of the first Oblate Sisters. The ox-waggon was one of those covered carts that rolls along light-heartedly and romantically only in the " Darkie " song or the Western Film, but in reality is a painful mode of travel indeed. " The waggon was a solid piece of work ", writes Father Davies, " but with no springs and of course no rubber tyres. The way was rough and hazardous, and the difficulty was that you never quite knew beforehand which wheel was going to strike a boulder, *which was inevitable*, or a tree, *which was unfortunate*. A moment of inattention, a rock under the wheel, and the occupants are flung into the air. They may land on something soft, they may land upon their neighbour's lap ; or, for such is the peril of the unexpected, they may land upon the corner of a packing case " . . . Every moment of their journey, therefore, must have been a painful one for these five Oblates. There was one particularly bad incident when the waggon broke down—perhaps it struck a tree—and Sister M. Colombe Balmelle was wounded in the head.

From angelic ministrations to the tender mercies of an ox-waggon ; and now, a civic reception—it was indeed a journey of contrasts. When the Sisters arrived at Kara-Agatch, a suburb of Adrianople, which was the residential district for the European colony, Father Galabert met them, and with him were the personnel of the French Consulate, and some prominent citizens, all on horseback. It was thus solemnly escorted, that the Sisters made their way through the streets of Adrianople to their new home, where a number of the ladies of the town had gathered to welcome them, and see to their needs. A big Turkish house was to be their new home, and the first focus of Oblate spiritual activity in the Near East. The aim of the Assumptionist Mission there was to bring back dissident Christians into the union of the Church. The first step towards this was the establishing of schools, as a preliminary move to the more effective measure later taken by the Fathers when they opened their *Bulgarian Seminary of Saint Peter and Saint Paul*, where youths were trained for the Priesthood in the Slav Rite, that they might become elements working towards Unity among their own people. Education, then, was to be the Sisters' first concern. On May 24th, 1868, they opened a Mission school under the patronage of Saint Vincent de Paul. These beginnings were made in great poverty, but they were blessed with the blessings given to those who are poor in spirit. A small boarding school for girls was soon added to this first venture, and it prospered. The following year, another school was opened in the district of Kaik, and here the Oblates had the splendid privilege of training in the Religious life a small group of convert Bulgarian Orthodox Nuns, with whom they studied Turkish, Bulgarian and Greek, three languages necessary for work on the Mission. The migration of the European colony to Kara-Agatch, led to the establishment of a day school there under the patronage of Saint Helen. This prospered in spite of the fulminations and anathemas of the Orthodox clergy against those who had sent their children to the Sisters. In the first months of the establishment, these anathemas would all but empty the school for a day or two, but the pupils would always come back. Even these sudden freezings of fear quickly ended, the anathema-hurling ceased, and the Sisters won their place, through their charity and intensive work, in the hearts of the people.

But this emphasis on educational work must not obscure the essential *pliability* which her Founder gave to the Oblate as one of the characteristics by which she was to be known. The circumstances of the time brought out this trait in these Missionary Sisters, and whenever things changed, or a new need arose, they were there to meet it. In 1871, for instance, the work of laying down a railroad joining Turkey with Bulgaria began in Kara-Agatch. Accidents multiplied, and there was no hospital to receive the wounded. Father Galabert called on the Oblates to take charge of a hospital which he had hastily set up in Kaik. Again during the Russo-Turkish war, the hospital and the school of Kaik were immediately put at the disposal of the governor of the town, and transformed into an ambulance depôt. The Oblates not only nursed the wounded, but they also welcomed the women and children who had remained behind after the evacuation of the town. The Sisters opened the gates of Heaven to the children who were dying in misery, and to a great number of refugees who were brought to them. The death-roll of war was increased by the ravages of exanthematic typhus and smallpox. Several of the nursing Oblates contracted the terrible disease, and two died victims of their devotion.

Peace came, and the Russian army made its entry into Constantinople. A new field of action opened up for the Oblates. The roads were strewn with abandoned children, some dead from starvation, some crushed under the trampling feet of panic-stricken refugees. A large number of bruised, bleeding, trampled and starving children were received and cared for by the Oblates. In a village called Armenli, some distance from Constantinople, a group of about fifty children, the eldest being scarcely ten years old, had taken refuge. When the Governor of Constantinople heard about this, he sent for these children. They were found abandoned to their own devices, grovelling in filth and devoured by lice. From time to time a piece of bread was flung to them, and they fought like dogs for it. It can be imagined in what a frightful condition they were when they reached Constantinople. The Governor asked Father Galabert to take charge of them, and he confided them to the Oblates. All this may be a little harsh on squeamish stomachs, but it is none the less salutary. When the Oblate says that her motto is *Ecce Ego, Mitte Me*—Here am I, send me—she really means what she says. It may be to teach in a school . . . or it may be to clean the lice-infested body of an abandoned child in whom, through the filth and stench, she sees a child of God. It was this dauntless and selfless spirit that called down a blessing on the spread of the Oblates' work in the East which continued to make headway against the prejudices of nations, and through the upheavals of war. Perhaps the surest token of that blessing was the presence of the cross. Between 1867 and the death of Father d'Alzon in 1880, the ranks of the Oblates were depleted by the death of no less than fifteen of the members. " The Oblates are filling Heaven " . . . was Father d'Alzon's remark on this. We must now consider some of those whose heroism laid down so generously the foundations on which the later magnificent work of the Oblates was built.

There was Mother Teresa, the leader of the first five pioneers. That she was chosen for this by Father d'Alzon himself is already a great tribute to her, for he was a connoisseur of greatness. She was a woman of deep interior life, who worked with all the energy of her being throughout those anxious and stormy days of the first Mission, and whose secret of vitality was her long nightly vigils before the Blessed Sacrament. Father Galabert recognized the foursquare qualities of great, practical holiness in her, and he learned to rely more and more on them. There seems to have been in her a balance between kindness and salutary rigour. There was never a flabby, characterless moment in her day's routine, and it was this same hard, ceaseless endeavour that she required from her Sisters. Nothing of the Jansenistic, however, had a place in her life, or in the atmosphere she created about her, for one of the things most remarked upon by the native peoples was the constant joy of these newcomers among them. It was inevitable that Mother Teresa should have worked in several places in the East, for her genius was called on to assist in several new ventures. For several years she directed the Community at Stamboul, and afterwards took charge of the house at Phanaraki. Her last work in the East was the direction of the Hospital of St. Louis, when age and weakness from long years of unremitting work made a decision for her which she herself would never have reached. From her sick-bed, she edified her

Sisters by her holiness, and to the end she continued to work to the utmost of her ever weakening physical power. It was fitting for a Daughter of Emmanuel d'Alzon that her hands should have been stretched out to work until they sank lifeless on the counterpane. This was the spirit of Mother Teresa, and when the gateway of Death opened finally to her, she crossed the threshold with the same calm and decisive step that had characterized all she had done on earth.

In 1872, Mother Veronica arrived at the Mission in the East to help Mother Teresa in the hard pioneer spade-work. Her assigned task was to assist in the direction of the hospital which was soon to be opened, and to take charge of the orphanage at Kara-Agatch. As one of the first six daughters of Father d'Alzon, and destined to be the last survivor, it was not extraordinary that she should have inherited from him the spirit of fearless, and—by all human standards—foolhardy faith which was so characteristic of him. In our final chapter we shall see with what earnestness and passionate intensity Father d'Alzon strove to impress his spirit on the Mother Foundress, and through her, on his Daughters. The life of Mother Veronica was one of the clear proofs that this spirit had taken root among them. Her faith was of that breath-taking illogical kind—illogical because it obeyed the laws of a higher logic—which would have delighted the heart of St. Francis of Assisi, and would certainly cause Father d'Alzon to say: " How delightfully foolish! How characteristic of a spiritual daughter of mine! "—or something similar. When for instance, she found that she had not enough money to pay for the flour she had already bought to feed her orphans, her solution was to go out, find another orphan and increase the total of hungry mouths by one. It was amazing how often this brought an answer, for when a person such as Mother Veronica does something of this kind, it is not tempting God, but rather making a loving challenge to Him. The work of the orphanage was very hard and very precarious. It was always difficult to make ends meet, and these ends had sometimes a disconcerting habit of suddenly moving much further apart.

There was the occasion during the Russo-Turkish war for

example, when word was brought to Mother Veronica that thirty orphaned and unwanted children were about to be thrown into the river. This was to be the cruel Oriental solution to the problem of providing for children whose parents had just been massacred. She did not hesitate a moment about sending word that a home was ready for them with her. " I acted ", she said to Father Galabert, " as you would have done in my place." Indeed, this was precisely what Father Galabert himself had done when he and his Fathers in Constantinople had not hesitated to undertake the care of orphans in similar circumstances. The news had brought an affectionate twinkle into Father d'Alzon's eyes when it reached him at Rome, and his comment was : " Father Galabert is looking after two hundred orphans. Just imagine Daddy Galabert handing round the feeding bottle ! It is simply delightful " . . . Behind the banter, was a proud appreciation of his spiritual son . . . This group swollen by waifs and strays collected here and there reached Mother Veronica, who now had a grand total of forty-five hungry mouths to feed.

How she managed to do it is little short of miraculous ; but one fact does emerge clearly, and this is that both she and her Sisters were content to line up behind their throng of orphans, and feed from the scrapings of the larder, if there was anything left to scrape. There is not a shadow of doubt that these early Oblates were often hungry because they gave the greater part of their own meagre ration to feed orphan children. How ironical, then, to find on record that a good lady, long accustomed to identify joy with material comforts, said to one of the Sisters : " Your Mother is always so gay. I hear that you have every-thing you want, and even manage to have a good time." It was a variant of the remark one so often hears, about Nuns having a peaceful life with no worries ! The reply was gracious, simple and shattering. " Madame, our food during the past few weeks has mainly consisted of a little garlic soup with a dish of greenstuff gathered from the field, and served either boiled or as a salad. We have no oil with it." Let us record in fairness that when the good lady recovered from her shock, she sent an alms to the Convent. One need not guess what happened to that alms—it was swallowed up in the orphans' flour bill, for the word " flour " must have been very frequently ringing all the changes of anxiety in the mind of Mother Veronica. When the supply was dangerously low, she would send the children to pray that some kind person would send money or flour. On one such occasion, a Catholic gentleman from the European quarter sent her two bags of flour. Such prompt response to her faith in the children's prayers was pretty regular, so that whenever she heard one of the children say to her : " We will ask God to send you some flour," she felt that all was well. This faith went hand in hand with her unremitting work, for no Daughter of Father d'Alzon could possibly confuse faith with lack of initiative and drive. Night after night she devoted herself to the making of artificial flowers, to embroidery and other fancy work, to be sold later to the ladies of the town that there might be money for flour. Besides her genius for orphan work, Mother Veronica was one of those who are gifted with a particularly gentle hand in dealing with the sick. She was a very intelligent woman with that true culture of the intellect that shows itself in gentleness and courtesy. That her skill and her faith were not in separate compartments was shown by the fact that when she had prepared her medicines, she invariably added a few drops of Lourdes water. There were many cures, and who is to say to what they are to be attributed ?—to the curative properties of the medicine, or to the few drops of this water dropped in with a fervent prayer and administered with a gentleness that itself had power to heal. It was this same gentleness and courtesy that led to her being welcomed into so many homes where, with magnificent tact, she re-established the practice of a religion long abandoned, regularized many marriages, arranged adult baptisms, and achieved many wonders of conversion through the power that is given to those who do all things sweetly . . . Mother Veronica's missionary work was interrupted by a period of some length when, having been recalled to France, she laboured with undiminished zeal in several of the Oblate convents there. When, driven out of France by the anti-clerical laws, she returned to the scene of her first vigorous years of service, she was feeling the weight of age and of sickness. For the last two years of her

life she was bedridden, but—again we remark the Oblate in her
—she continued to help in every way she could, and towards
the end, when there was nothing more she could do, her fingers
were still busy making flowers and preparing linen for the altar.
Her death was gentle, like that of those she had so often helped to
die. It was on February 2nd, 1900, and her Sisters were intoning
in choir the canticle in the Office of Compline: "Now Thou
dost dismiss thy servant, O Lord, according to Thy word—in
peace."

These two magnificent women—Mother Teresa and Mother
Veronica—were the great moral and spiritual pillars of strength
to the extremely difficult Mission undertaken by the Oblates.
They had both received the spiritual impress of Father d'Alzon ;
his spirit lived in them, and the little Community looked to them
as their models, imitated them, drew courage and inspiration
from them. They rise as giants of holiness from the very cradle
of the Oblates, and their challenge is flung forward into the
years to all those who have enlisted, or ever shall enlist, under
the standard of Emmanuel d'Alzon.

We turn from them to consider another of the pioneer Sisters
—this time a humble and heroic Greek girl, Maria Roussou,
born in April, 1890. This date may seem too late for the term
" pioneer " to be applied to her, but we use it, because she was
a shining example of the native heroism in these mission lands.
For is it not one of the supreme tests of a missionary endeavour
that it should win from the native people, those who will be
shining dynamic examples to their own race ? At the age of
eighteen, Maria joined the Oblates and became Sister Eftykia,
(Hope). She was soon outstanding among her companions
by her devotion to duty, and her intense desire to do her full
share towards achieving Christian unity. This flame of
Christian charity was intensified by her pure and lofty patriotism,
and it leaped up hungrily when she saw the chance of showing
her devotion. In Constantinople, there is the large yellow
quadrangular, window-studded barracks of Selimieh, whose
massive proportions loom large above the steep rocky coast
bordering the sea. Here, after the disturbances in Anatolia in
September, 1922, more than 15,000 Greek refugees found a

temporary home. Overcrowding and bad conditions, coupled with the famine of the severe winter of 1923, soon loosed a prairie fire of disease among them. The estimated death-roll was 250 to 300 victims every week. The Pope furnished the means of supplying a daily distribution of soup to 500 small children among the refugees, and once again, the onerous task of distributing it was given to the Oblates. To volunteer for the work was in all probability equivalent to signing one's own death warrant. It was a supreme moment for testing the spirit of the Oblates, and they did not fail. Volunteers came forward— and among them the thirty-three year old Sister Eftykia; her superiors hesitated : she was so young and inexperienced ! But no one could plead for life as Sister Eftykia pleaded for this almost certain death. "I entered the Assumption", she urged, "to help in the cause of Christian unity, and here is my chance of doing so" . . . "There are many other ways of helping the Church", countered her Superior. "For instance, you have just completed the instruction of a Greek Orthodox from Cadi-Keni whose conversion must have been a great joy to you" . . . "Yes mother," Sister Eftykia still pleaded, "but I feel an overwhelming desire to go to the assistance of these unfortunate people. They are my people and speak my language, and I know their habits and customs. Four of my brothers fought to deliver them from the Turks in Asia Minor, and one of them died in captivity".

As one reads this, one sees the eager face lifted in humble and ardent entreaty, the pleading in the eyes. Her enthusiasm wrung an uneasy consent from her Superior, and Sister Eftykia went eagerly and joyfully towards that cess of disease as another might go to a garden of roses. Without a thought for disease or danger, she moved blithely among these her people, finding here some lapsed, there some children for First Communion; again some girls wishing to be instructed in the Catholic Faith . . . and she could see that the more she explored, the more she would find to do and the more goodwill she would discover among these poor unfortunates. It was sheer intoxication for Sister Eftykia, and there in the midst of fetid disease, she experienced the purest joy. Suddenly the hand of death was upon her; despite the precautions taken, she had contracted typhus; and yet one feels that no precautions could possibly have been proof against the enthusiasm with which this nun set about the dire work for which she had pleaded so earnestly. She herself was the first to diagnose it, and she went calmly to her Superior and said : " I have come from the barracks, where I have certainly caught typhus; I feel that it will be fatal. I know that in this disease the brain is affected and the mind does not usually function clearly, so I should like to make my Confession, while it is possible for me to do so " . . . Her agony soon set in, and lasted six days. In her delirium, her mind wandered in sorrow over the little faults of her life; and at the end she spoke again of the dream that had filled her few short years of life : " I do so wish with all my heart that nothing of my sacrifice may be lost for the Unity of the Churches " . . . It has been well said that works founded on such deaths do not perish !

These few examples from the early years of the Oblate mission field will serve, more than volumes of comment, to show how the ideals of the Assumption came alive in these Daughters of Father d'Alzon. He had brought all the richness of his maturity to the Oblates, and they had learned quickly and well. He had stamped their origins with his own virile sanctity, his spirit of initiative, his thirst for good works, and it was all this that the world met in the Oblates of the Assumption.

There are Oblates today who remember those early Sisters when their evening had come and the shadows of life were lengthening. They remember them as old and feeble, bent under the weight of their years, weakened by their life of heroic toil. To the young novices, they were " the old Sisters ", pottering about, ceaselessly praying; they were among those who lived on the other rim of life. Then some novice, meeting one of them, praying her slow way in the garden, would say : " Mother, you knew Father d'Alzon, didn't you ? " At the sound of that name, a strange and beautiful transformation would occur in the old Sister. She would straighten, as if her youth had suddenly come alive in her again; her eyes would flash with

for fifty years could no longer measure up to it. "He has no disease," said the doctor, when his brethren anxiously questioned him. "All the organs are sound, but they are the organs of a man of ninety, not those of a man of seventy." He said as much to d'Alzon : "Your health is like an exhausted capital"—and for answer he had received a hearty laugh and one of those quips that so often rippled through the language of Father d'Alzon : "Well, I have exhausted quite a few of those in my life, so I might as well exhaust *that*". That capital was indeed running out. He appointed Father Picard his successor, and let his life sink more and more into contemplation and prayer, that he might create within himself a peace which would merge with eternity. By November, he had taken to his bed, never to rise again. Father Emmanuel Bailly administered the last Sacraments to him, and during the next two weeks he said goodbye to those whose lives he had lifted and made great in the sight of the angels. The bed he lay on was not his own, for it was only in those last few days that he consented to rest on something softer than his hard plank. On November 16th, the great scene of farewells took place, when Father Picard presented all the religious available for the final blessings of their beloved Father. When Father d'Alzon raised his tired eyes to look at his assembled sons, they must have rested with particular affection on Father Hippolyte Saugrain, the poor grinder at grammar who had become a cornerstone of the Assumption, and who was now privileged to be the only one of that first 1850 group present at the passing of his Father. They heard the halting voice that was all that remained of the vigorous cut and thrust of their Father ; and in the hush, they felt each word trembling with the emotion that filled to overflowing the heart of this lion of the Cévennes, this man of the regal head and the seraphic soul. "*My brethren, you know that after God and the Blessed Virgin, I have loved you most on earth . . . We are going to leave each other . . . Submission to God's will . . . He is the Master . . . I am going, but my heart will stay with you*". On that same day, at nine o'clock in the morning, Mother Emmanuel-Marie of the Compassion came and knelt at the threshold of his room. He blessed her and all her daughters. In that moment, behind those tired eyes looking at her, may not the years have rolled back, so that again he was looking at the little girl who did not fail him ? He lingered on for a few days, and we are fortunate in having an eye-witness account of his death which shows indeed how men like Emmanuel d'Alzon die : " His hand was raised in blessing to the very end, and during the long prayers for the dying, his hand grasped the lighted blessed candle. Then his Religious recited the Rosary . . . and when they had finished the fourth decade of the Glorious Mysteries, *the Assumption*, he spoke his last word, and that was : " My Jesus." It was midday on the feast of the Presentation of Our Lady in the Temple . . . and the bells were ringing the Angelus ".

The axe had already splintered the door of the Assumption in Paris to expel his Religious in the name of masonic hate ; but he knew nothing of this. Nor did he know that only his own death agony had suspended that same axe raised to smash the door of the College at Nîmes. His dead hand was effective in suspending it for some time after his death, for the Prefect of Police said he was afraid it would cause riots in the streets. Let that be recorded as a tribute, unwillingly wrung from an enemy, to the power of Emmanuel d'Alzon even in death.

The final detail to complete the picture of this glorious death, comes from Mother Emmanuel-Marie of the Compassion. " On the evening of that day," she writes, " an extraordinary thing happened. A light of fire, in the form of a heart, suddenly appeared in my cell. It rose to a height of about a metre and a half. Its motion was slow, very slow, and left me with a peaceful feeling. A week later, I told this to Father Emmanuel Bailly. He was struck by the occurrence, and asked me if I could give the precise time. It was between 7 p.m. and 7.14 p.m. ' What a curious coincidence ! ' he answered. ' The Religious (at the College) were just then finishing the chanting of the Office of the Dead ! ' "

At no time in her life was Mother Emmanuel-Marie a dreamer. There is no reason why we cannot accept her word, and wonder with her about it. She herself was convinced that this extraordinary event was a sign that the Founder had entered Heaven. It may well have been ; and if so, what a beautiful final gesture of assurance that he would always be with them, to his beloved Daughters, the spiritual children of his maturity—those spiritual souls into whom he had instilled his courage, his heroism, and ideals of sefless service.

THE IDEAL OF TOTAL ADAPTABILITY IN PRACTICE

IN THE FINAL chapter of this book, it will be seen how Father d'Alzon laid down an ideal of complete adaptablility for his Oblates. They were to be completely " offered up "—their very name said so—to the needs of the Church in whatever part of the world they found themselves. An ideal such as this demands a spirit of total selflessness ; and it is a gripping thing to see that spirit incarnated in his Daughters, to feel its breath in every deed of their heroic lives. In the silent archives of every Congregation are the brief records of many heroic souls whose lives will never be presented to the public. They were not those with the ten talents, but those with the three, the two, the one ; and if, as is inevitable, it is the achievements of the ten-talented that are sung—if only the names of the great ones are brought forward—it must be remembered that in the darkness behind the light shed on them, are the many others, without whose example and humble co-operation, they might not have reached the heights. They are but the crest of the wave, and that wave is the heroism of many. Or—to adapt the metaphor of Christ : " by their fruits you shall know them "—we are merely selecting the finest on the laden tree, and savouring their heroism as samples of the spiritual ripeness that is all. With these preliminary words, we turn the pages that record the lives of one or two of the great ones whose talents allowed them to live the Oblate ideal on heroic lines.

Among the names that claim immediate attention, is that of Mother Jeanne de Chantal. Born in 1848, she had all the dash and verve that characterises the people of the *Midi* ; and when, at the age of sixteen, she experienced what she later called her " conversion ", it was merely that she diverted her intense love for dance and song and laughter, her thirst for living, into an intense and joyful pursuit of holiness and of self-oblation. She

was an extremely beautiful girl with dark brown eyes ; her conversation was spiced with a quickness and wit which her strong
southern accent seemed to enhance.   When, at the age of twenty,
she at last obtained the tardy consent of her parents, her leanings
were towards the contemplative life of the Carmel ; but a friend
of Father d'Alzon considered that the mixed life of contemplation and apostolic action was more in keeping with her temperament, and accordingly directed her to Father d'Alzon.   She
went to Nîmes and offered herself as an Oblate ; but no sooner
had she done so than she became a prey to agonizing doubts.
" Mother," she said to Mother Correnson, " I have no vocation.
I must leave immediately in order to console my father on whom
I have brought useless sorrow."   Mother Correnson reasoned
with her in vain, and then brought her to Father d'Alzon.
" Very good," he said, " you will leave, but in a few days, when
you and I shall both have had time to decide clearly that you
have no vocation.   In three days, you will come back to
me, and we shall decide then."   Before the three days had
passed, Sister Jeanne de Chantal felt that the Oblate ideas
and ideals were indeed those of her own life ; or, as she expressed it in her last years : " I have always been happy in the
Assumption."

The years pass, and we find her in the mission field of the
East, among the intrepid Oblate pioneers.   That vigour and
energy that demanded dance and laughter and song were still
there, but had now a new, a magnificent outlet ; those dark and
shining eyes called forth the admiration of the Turkish women
—*Ne guzel kara gueux !* (What beautiful eyes!) they used to say—
but they were beautiful with the tranquillity of grace and alive
with apostolic zeal.   Mother Jeanne de Chantal had come as superior of the seventh group of Oblates sent out in the first five years
of the Eastern Mission.   Her stay in the East coincided with the
hardships and the miseries which accompanied the Russo-Turkish
war.   She led her Sisters bravely along the hard way of sacrifice
and of starvation which they were called upon to tread, when the
needs of destitute orphans demanded all their energy and resources.
Her first sojourn in the East ended with her recall to France by
Father Picard who wished her to take charge of the new noviciate

at Sèvres. It was good that the young Sisters should have as their guide, one who had been formed under the direct influence of Father d'Alzon, and whose spirit was his spirit. Were this a life of Mother Jeanne de Chantal, full justice might be done to her work at Sèvres; in the foundation of the historic convent at 20, Cours-la-Reine, Paris; her educational work; the devotion and self-sacrifice of her second and third sojourns in the East. But space forces us to hasten on, that we may give our attention to that aspect of her life which must surely grip the reader's imagination and stir his enthusiasm, her work at Bagnolet.

At the outbreak of the First World War, when the Sisters were forced to leave Turkey, Mother Jeanne de Chantal returned to Paris. She was then sixty-six years old, but time had not taken away her vigour, and a work of splendid heroism awaited her. In every big city, there are certain areas where the dregs of society accumulate, where plague-spots of immorality and crime are many, and where human nature smothers all that is best in it, to become what Pascal said human nature could indeed be—" a cesspool." Such an area was the district between Bagnolet and Montreuil. The centre of the district was a gaming house, old, tumbling down, held together in makeshift fashion, patched with pieces of broken boxes. Around it were the hovels of the poor; makeshift lodgings of old tin scrap and flattened biscuit tins hammered haphazardly together. Into this squalor, people were born, lived, died like animals, without priest or prayer. The priest, "the black man," was regarded as enemy number one, and the name of Christ was simply a curse.

It was into this muddy swirl of filth and hatred and bitterness and blasphemy, that Mother Jeanne de Chantal came intrepidly to preach by word and example the charity of Christ. The first objects of this charity were the unhappy children whose souls were being corrupted by the terrible conditions into which they were born. Mother de Chantal and her two companions opened a school and a dispensary, and announced that they intended to visit the homes of the poor. They established a chapel in which Mass was said every Sunday. News of this got around, and these black and bitter inhabitants of Bagnolet, who would have spat their contempt at the mere sight of a cassock, accepted the priests who now said Mass there, because they were soldier-priests dressed in the uniform of their country. The adult congregation at Sunday Mass increased more and more, as these Sisters visited house after house inviting these unfortunates to come to the marriage feast. "Come on Sunday, then, and pray with us," they would say, "and you will see how much stronger you will be after that to bear your burdens and your sufferings." The poor are quick to recognize sincerity, and they knew that in these Sisters they had real friends. When they visited the miserable dens these people called "homes", mercy, compassion and the charity of Christ crossed the threshold with them and became a warmth in the cold heart of these people's lives. Little by little, that warmth spread from family to family; and just as a smile can soften the hard lines of depression and anger in a human face, so this warmth changed the face of Bagnolet. When these poor wretches made their first, awkward, rather shame-faced way to the new chapel, they were greeted by a splendid vision of flowers decorating the altar, of nicely arranged curtains, of a hundred little loving touches which, though the materials available were poor and scanty, the Sisters had been at infinite pains to provide, so that even the very room would speak a colourful welcome. The children sang for them, and they themselves soon joined in the singing as only a group of Frenchmen can. This great concern for detail which marked the work of the Sisters, also showed itself in the improved conditions of the children, who now began to be somewhat cleaner and more tidily dressed—an indication that mothers were at last becoming alive to their duties.

Several incidents have been put on record which show Mother Jeanne de Chantal in full apostolic action. There was the moment, for example, when a man of very unpleasant aspect came to her to ask her to assist his wife who was seriously ill. The Sisters went to her, and discovered that she was an ex-star of one of the most famous cafés. Her years had been linked each to each by song and dance and the laughter of life; but the last time religion had touched the hem of her life was in the dim past when she had made her First Communion. When Mother

Jeanne de Chantal had attended fully to all her wants, she spoke to her about her soul. It was a strange word, like a word spoken in an unknown language, to the unfortunate woman. The soul meant religion—and religion was something that went with clean linen and being well-to-do, and had no place in Bagnolet. Slowly, with infinite patience, as one guides the feet of an awakening sleep-walker, Mother Jeanne explained how religion was none of these things, and how the Kingdom of Heaven and its eternal happiness would soon be hers in return for sorrow and a prayer. It was hard to kindle again that childhood faith smothered by the moral squalor of Bagnolet; but success at last crowned the efforts and prayers of the Sisters. It is an eloquent comment on the district and the conditions in which these Sisters worked, that, when they went to summon a priest to the woman's bedside, he answered : " It is impossible for me to show myself in those quarters in broad daylight. I would not get through alive . . . I shall come to-night, and take with me my sacristan armed with a cudgel to defend ourselves if the need arises." These words made the Sisters themselves realize for the first time what dangers they themselves had been running, among this horde of de-humanized fugitives from justice, social outcasts, deserters, the scum of every nation. But it was this fearless innocence that had been about them like a protective cloak, and they had never been molested. Its reward was such a moment as this, when they knelt by the bedside of a soul they had saved from the slime, and watched her fervently receiving her God and then dying in peace to meet the merciful judgment of that same God to Whom she had given her heart when the shadow of death was already upon her.

Then, coming closely on this incident, was the moment when Mother Jeanne de Chantal met a young man of thirty, a human skeleton coughing himself to death and supporting himself gropingly along a wall. She spoke softly and compassionately to him, and he allowed her to assist him to his hovel. Her promise to return immediately loosed a protest : " No, no, don't bother. I have all I want—and I have a confessor at Montreuil who will do all that is necessary in due course." Mother Jeanne was too wise to believe in this imaginary confessor conveniently produced by the unfortunate morphino-maniac. Two days later she was again on his doorstep, her bag brimming with good things—wine, biscuits, fruit, linen. Her kindness and patience, strengthened by the prayers of her Sisters and her own ceaseless prayer, won their way to the heart of this unfortunate man. Where only blasphemy had lived on his lips, she now had the joy of hearing the *Ave Maria* and the prayer of sorrow; she saw the hard bitter pride within him softening to receive his Eucharistic Lord, and when death came, it claimed a son of God, and not a braggart of the malodorous *bande à Bonnot*, a notorious gang of thieves and murderers in 1912. The joy that this brought to Mother Jeanne de Chantal must surely have been heightened by the knowledge that she was the instrument of God in answering a good woman's prayer. She learned from the patient that his mother was a poor street-sweeper, who plied her brush hour after hour, and accompanied it with a ceaseless stream of *Aves* rising to the feet of the Mother of God to beg mercy for her erring son. The prayers of this other Monica in the dust and garbage of a slum street, had received a magnificent answer.

Mother Jeanne de Chantal came to Bagnolet in 1915, at the age of sixty-seven; she continued there until her death in 1936, at the age of eighty-eight. It is absolutely amazing that such a spirit of energy and of drive should have been found in one so advanced in years, and it shows how vividly the dynamic ideas of Father d'Alzon lived in her. Those twenty-one years saw a complete change in Bagnolet; and to-day, as an organized parish, where the Oblates run an infants' school, a Kindergarten and a huge dispensary, Bagnolet has almost forgotten that it was once a little kingdom of vice. But the intrepid pioneer who walked in fearlessly where a priest could go only under cover of darkness, is not forgotten. Her magnificent work in that district was a fitting crown to a splendid apostolic career. In her whole life as an Oblate, she embodied supremely the ideal of selfless service, of complete adaptability which Father d'Alzon had laid down for his Daughters.

We must now deal with the famous *La Bonne Presse*, which embodies one of the master ideas of Father d'Alzon—the apostolate of the pen. It was founded by that magnificent son of his, Father Vincent de Paul Bailly, the Journalist Monk of the Assumption, the man who put so vividly what the aims of every Catholic newspaper should be : " *Take the demon of publicity,*" he wrote, " *harness him to the things of the spirit, and sprinkle him with holy water till he howls.*" Thanks to the magnificent efforts of Father Vincent de Paul, worthy son of that Bailly who was the co-founder of the St. Vincent de Paul Society, the *Bonne Presse* is to-day the most powerful force in French Catholic journalism. It publishes the famous Parisian daily : *La Croix* ; it publishes periodicals with a yearly circulation of 300,000,000 ; it sends out a steady stream of worth-while Catholic books. The story of the *Bonne Presse* and its founder has been splendidly told by that modern Journalist of the Assumption, Father Gabriel Slater. Our concern here is to show the part played by the Oblates in making this great achievement possible.

The first women associated with the heroic beginnings of the *Bonne Presse*, were a few pious ladies and girls who busied themselves in a little room of the Avenue Montaigne, in folding and dispatching the *Croix-Revue* and the now famous family weekly : *Le Pèlerin*. Their leader was later destined to become an Oblate, Sister Saint-Jean, and to give a life of splendid service. But when, in 1883, *La Croix* began to appear as a daily paper, more commodious apartments were required, and a two-storeyed house at 20, Cours-la-Reine was taken over. It was at this stage that the formal association of the Oblates with the Press began. Two of the Sisters, proficient in typography and in proof-correction, instructed their companions in this apostolate so entirely new to them. Here again we meet that adaptability which is the keynote of the Oblate ideal : this is the work to be done, and we must learn to do it. Soon they were augmented by lay employees, and when the work became too extensive for the premises, they moved in 1884 to the premises of Gustave Doré, 3 rue Bayard, and finally to number 5. The premises were enlarged by the addition of a chapel and two storeys in 1886, one for typography and the other for the folding and dispatch of periodicals. The following year saw the end of the period when printing was done by an outside firm ; machinery was installed, and the *Bonne Presse* came of age.

Besides its primary aim of fighting the irreligious and anti-clerical press, the *Bonne Presse* was a pioneer in the social work of establishing truly Christian workshops. Its staff grew to a high total of 300 administrative employees and some 400 workers, both men and women, who were provided with a working atmosphere which was morally excellent and of a high religious tone. This does not mean that the *Bonne Presse* is something starched stiff with piety. When I was privileged to visit the Press recently, I was struck by the atmosphere of joy that pervades it. It is a hive of high-pressure industry, machines humming, fingers moving deftly setting type, folding, dispatching, addressing—every activity highly and actively organized ; and through it all runs that current of Christian joy one feels in every department. In the heart of the *Bonne Press* is the Blessed Sacrament, as the inspiration of all its activity, The Oblates move among the workers, wearing habits specially designed to suit their work ; they live and pray in their convent at the top of the building, and come down each day to work assiduously side by side with their lay companions. Their task is to direct and forward the work in every way ; but they devote themselves with equal zeal to the care of the young girl employees by providing opportunities for receiving the Sacraments, by organizing weekly courses in religion given by one of the Fathers, and by themselves holding classes in French and in Catechism for the apprentices, as well as organizing a yearly retreat about Eastertide. They also provide for their temporal needs. The sick are taken to a doctor and are often nursed with maternal care. Those whom sickness compels to remain at home for a time, are visited and comforted by the Sisters, and receive their pay during such absences. Convalescence in the country air is even arranged for those whose families cannot afford it. It is clear, therefore, that the work of the Oblates in the *Bonne Press* is much more than wholehearted co-operation in the apostolate of the pen. It is a social work, a work of compassion, a lever for the spiritual and temporal uplift of working conditions. It provides a fine opportunity for the Oblate really to live her name—to be as one who is " offered " for the fulfilment of the thousand needs to which such an undertaking can give rise. The proof of success in meeting this manifold challenge was the number of Oblate vocations that came from among the first workers in the *Bonne Presse*. This was not surprising when it is remembered that the Mother Superior was Mother Marie de la Croix, who, in any account of the Oblates, must be singled out for more than a passing mention in connection with that Press.

Born in 1854, Mother Marie de la Croix became an Oblate in her thirty-third year, and spent the last thirty years of her life, until her death in 1919, as Mother Superior of the Oblate Community of the *Bonne Presse*. She brought to her delicate task of pioneer work a deep piety, a thirst for real achievements, and an enmity to anything that savoured of empty show. Her thirty years of devotion to the work of the Press were thirty years of assiduous attention to the smallest details. No one ever heard her complain of tiredness or over-work; she was at once a woman of steel and a woman of warm human affection; heart and head and every ounce of physical energy were given to her work. Yet, despite her years of heaped-up activity, hers was a life of intense prayer. Despite the number of matters clamouring for her attention, she managed to say the whole Divine Office daily. Father Bailly knew her worth; as her biographer has so aptly said, " to put any work into her hands was equivalent to saying : *Fiat Lux* . . . ." let light and power come to this undertaking ! The workers soon learned to love her for her sincerity and her genuine anxiety for all that concerned their welfare. To her must be given the credit for that family atmosphere that still lives in the *Bonne Presse*. She organized those little " treats " for the employees that mean so much in the creation of such an atmosphere. After the Christmas Midnight Mass, for instance, she used to organize a supper, followed by two draws for presents. The first was a genuine draw; the second was cleverly manipulated so that each got a suitable present. Father Bailly tells how he himself, when introducing these draws, said : " My friends, we shall now have two draws : the first a serious one, and the other . . ." At which point, Mother Marie, anxious for the fate of her amiable little tricks, whispered : " and the other equally so." It was this atmosphere of home and of homely fun that she succeeded in creating, which was responsible for the fine spirit among the workers of the *Bonne Presse.*

The years passed, and *La Croix* became a power to be reckoned with in France. In a few weeks, it had succeeded in raising two million francs in voluntary subscriptions for the dome of the Sacré Coeur in Montmartre. The radical deputies became alarmed ; what could not this paper do in raising colossal funds for any political party it chose to support ? Already, the powerful electoral organization built up by the Catholics was causing alarm. A law was passed which was tantamount to the strangling of religious life. After a series of Machiavellian moves, all the houses of the Fathers of the Assumption were invaded by magistrates and police, and taken over at eight o'clock in the morning November 11th, 1899.

The group who walked unceremoniously into the *Bonne Presse* and mounted the stairs towards the Convent quarters, found the commanding figure of Mother Marie de la Croix standing on the stairs, and bringing the invaders to a halt with a gesture of imperious command. Walking fearlessly towards them, she firmly pointed out to their leader the illegality of " unleashing these men like a pack of dogs " in a peaceful convent, without first producing a mandate, if he had one, for being in the place at all. Cowed by her dignified firmness, the commissioner stuttered some excuses, produced his mandate, and asked her to be so kind as to assist him in the examination he was obliged to make of the papers in her desk. Mother Marie herself took complete charge, and the commissioner, feeling like a chidden schoolboy and uncomfortable under the calm gaze of this quietly masterful woman, conducted his sorry business with what semblance of dignity he could muster. Meantime, the police were questioning each of the Sisters, examining everything in the house, even the poor furnishing of the cells, whose poverty and bareness, more than anything else they met with in the *Bonne Presse,* made them feel there was not a rag of dignity left to them in the discharge of this ignoble duty.

The French government dealt a cunning blow to the Assumptionists by a disingenuous promise to Pope Leo XIII that no proceedings would be taken against the other Congregations if Father Bailly and his companions would relinquish the editorship of *La Croix*. The ruse was successful, and at a time when the persecuted Fathers might naturally have expected a letter of compassionate sympathy from Rome, in its place came one to the French government accepting their promise and, " in the interests of peace," acceding to their request. " Father Bailly's pen was broken too," writes his biographer, Lacoste. But he submitted. Having assembled the staff, he told them that God was demanding from him the sacrifice of his Isaac ; that he must needs obey. On April 1st, 1900, *La Croix* was sold to M. Paul Feron-Vrau, a valiant Catholic and friend of the Fathers. To continue their work, the Sisters were compelled to relinquish their religious habit, and to find scattered lodgings outside their Convent. Their little chapel stood empty, the Blessed Sacrament gone ; and it became a place of prayer only when one of the Sisters slipped into it to fulfil as best she could, her religious duties. It was extremely difficult for the Sisters to keep in touch with the Superior ; each was left to her own devices in leading her religious life—assisting at morning Mass in the nearest church, fitting in her other religious duties at various times during her working day, leading both a secular and a religious life, not allowing the latter to obtrude too much while at the same time she kept herself unspotted from the world. It was a period of great trial and sorrow for those Sisters, and the manner in which they met its challenge showed what splendid religious they were. Mother Marie de la Croix went under her family name of Rose Jouet, but it was a case, as Horace would say, of changing the name but not the sky. At no time in her history, perhaps, was she such a valiant woman of God and of the Cross.

In 1905, the law allowed the chapel of the *Bonne Presse* to be re-established. The crucifix was replaced on the tabernacle, and with the enthroning of the Crucified, a part of its normal spiritual life returned to the *Bonne Presse*. With the installation of new machinery, the growth of staff and the purchase of new premises, her work grew more and more heavy. She gave herself unstintingly to every demand made on her energy and her work-taut hours. The design of this book does not allow us to follow any further details in the life of Mother Marie ; but sufficient has been said to show how " the big spirit " of Emmanuel d'Alzon lived in her to make her one of the giant souls of the Assumption.

We turn now to the story of the coming of the Oblates to England fifty years ago. In July, 1903, they landed in England and established themselves in Charlton. Anyone visiting Charlton to-day will find a very well-established parish under the devoted ears of the Fathers of the Assumption, a fine church, and beside it the solid block of the guest-house, convent and schools of the Oblates of the Assumption. It was to no such smoothly running conditions that the pioneer Sisters came, but rather, to all the rigour of a foreign mission. There were no Fathers ; there was no church ; there was no school. There was simply a large house, into which nothing had entered for several years except seepy, dirt-laden London fog, which seemed indeed to have taken up its permanent abode there if one could judge from the filthy brown of the walls which darkened the whole house even at midday. The house itself was, needless to say, in a state of indescribable dirt and neglect, and absolutely empty of furniture. This was the grim welcome that greeted the Sisters when they turned the key for the first time and went into their new home. Their first scanty meal was taken sitting on the grass in front of the house—" an English picnic " they called it. Later, a van completed its journey by water and land from Bordeaux to London, and came lumbering up with what poor possessions the Sisters had managed to bring with them. Father d'Alzon had said it was a good thing that the beginnings of the Oblates in Le Vigan should have been marked with the poverty of Bethlehem. He would therefore have approved of the conditions in which the English mission began, and he would have regarded them as an earnest of success. He would have recognized, too, the spirit he had given to his Oblates, in the way these Sisters faced up to the manifold difficulties awaiting them.

" Disponibilité totale "—complete adaptability—this was what he asked of his Oblates, whether in the workrooms of the Press, the dispensaries of the Missions, hunting for souls in the slums of Paris, or scraping congealed London Fog off the walls of a damp house. Eager hands went out to help with the unloading; and the following day, those same hands were busy sweeping, cleaning, washing, vigorously scrubbing the largest and best room in order that Holy Mass might be celebrated there as soon as possible. The ceiling had to be renewed, the walls cleaned, and at last, the longed-for moment came when the Sisters could kneel in their own chapel in the midnight silence, and join with Father Benedict in blessing a room for the Master. The following morning, to their intense joy, the first Mass was celebrated. The altar was a temporary, makeshift one of packing cases and planks covered with light hangings; the Tabernacle was of simple white wood, decorated with appropriate paintings. God did not see the poverty of the surroundings for the warm fervour of the prayers that mounted to Him. Further improvements were gradually made; the walls were decorated, and an oak altar was sent from France.

The first sign that the coming of the Sisters had been noticed in Charlton was the arrival of two Irishmen, the grocer and his brother, to assist at Mass on their first Sunday there. The following Sunday the attendance had increased to six; it rose steeply to thirty and continued to increase. In spite of every effort to use every inch of space, the Chapel was soon too small, and the communicating door into another room had to be opened. Home-made kneelers and school desks were used. There was an early Mass and Communion, followed later by a High Mass, and Vespers were sung in the evening. After Vespers, and whatever the weather, the Sisters had to set to work and carry all the provisional benches to a neighbouring stable. On Sundays, they themselves assisted at Mass by huddling together on the threshold of the door that led on to the altar through the small temporary parlour and sacristy.

The weekdays were filled with hard work. The only workman called in to help the Sisters for an hour or two was the plumber. Otherwise, it was the Sisters themselves who became sweeps, ceiling painters, paper hangers and general decorators. Great progress was made in an atmosphere of joyful activity. While working, they recited the Rosary together, and sang hymns; but these were sometimes interrupted by a wholehearted burst of laughter as an unwary amateur house-painter splashed her neighbour with paint, or a too enthusiastic paper-hanger included herself in the area to be covered. The prayers were none the less fervent for that, and there was a fine bravery about it all. Father Benedict attended the evening recreations, and gave them lessons in English. In spite of all their work, the Sisters recited the Divine Office before the Blessed Sacrament exposed ; and this was followed by Benediction.

Winter came swiftly, as an English winter can. The house was bitterly cold and thoroughly damp ; there was not one door or window which fastened properly, and so every room and corridor was an eddy of chill draughts. There was no coal, and no money to buy coal. But there were some trees away at the bottom of the hill. Father Benedict chopped some of them to serve as fuel. The Sisters tied ropes to the giant logs and dragged them up the steep incline. There were blistered hands and aching backs—but the same joy in the task. It is only when one stands to-day to look at that steep incline, that one realizes just what that ideal of complete adaptability meant in heroic practice. The same spartan conditions marked the beginnings of their educational work in Charlton.

In October, the first two pupils arrived, and with them the Private School began. But it was soon absolutely necessary to provide for the less wealthy by establishing a Parish school. There was an old greenhouse situated behind what was later to become the Sanctuary of the present church, and the Sisters converted this into a kindergarten. The older children were installed in one of the largest rooms in the house itself ; but as their numbers increased, it became necessary to take over an old stable where the marks of the swishing tails of horses were still plainly on the walls. Here a class for the boys was set up. It had been uphill work from the moment of arrival, and there was no softness or comfort about it all, but stern endurance. Yet, when this much had been achieved, the Sisters supplemented their work with visits to the sick and the poor, thus paving the way for the ministry of the Fathers.

This is not the place to stir the dust that has settled on old unhappy far-off things ; suffice it to say that the archives could tell a sad tale. A revival of Catholicism was not welcomed. Weaving tongues spun their web of mischief about a school in a greenhouse and a barn. Orders came that the school was to be closed. It was then that the parishioners rose to protest loudly in favour of the Sisters' work. A certain Mr. Jukes launched an appeal to all the Catholics in the parish; meetings were held to discuss the matter, and all voted in favour of the school. A petition was drawn up, and, together with the promise to build a suitable school, was forwarded to the Board of Education. The cause was won.

Two outstanding Mother Superiors on the English mission call for special mention : Mother Michael and Mother Mary of the Compassion. Mother Michael, immediately on profession, had been sent to the Near East, and had opened new houses on both sides of the Bosphorus. Her attitude towards the Turks showed both intelligence and penetration; she said that the "simplest way" to meet their wildness is "to tell them the truth." When the Turks burned down her convent, and threw down all her work in the dust, she assembled her Sisters and sang the *Magnificat*. Such was the spirit she brought with her to Charlton, where she was Mother Superior during the 1914-1918 War. Not the least of her tasks was the great personal one of gaining a knowledge of English. Even when huddled in the shelters during air-raids, she would still be found busily thumbing the dictionary and learning to read; so that, had it pleased Divine Providence to claim her as a war victim, she would have been interrupted by death at her task of pursuing the ideal of total adapability. Hardly six weeks after her arrival, she was able to address the pupils at morning assembly, and they followed perfectly her clear and carefully enunciated English. She took the English to her heart, in the true missionary spirit of being " all things to all men "; just as she was to be Yugoslav with the Yugoslavs when she was sent to Beograd after the war to open a convent there and build a huge school She was to come back many times to Charlton, as Superior General, and she gave the Sisters there the benefit of her shrewd advice in matters concerning the building of the new school and convent.

The Charlton parish has developed into one of the most

vigorous in London, and at the hub of its activity is the Assumption Convent. Their original convent has become the Fathers' Priory, and they themselves, after several moves, have established themselves in their present spacious building, where they conduct a school which has won a well-deserved reputation for thorough-going efficiency.

The second Superior at Charlton : Mother Mary of the Compassion was a woman of quiet aristocratic temperament and of great holiness, whose task it was to make the best of the few poor amenities of those early years. Some time before, she had been in charge of an orphanage in the slums of Nîmes, from whence she had been summoned for an unexpected task. Indeed, her name holds an honoured place in the early history of the *Orantes*—the contemplative branch of the Assumption.

It has been seen that spiritual ties linked together the various independent branches of the Assumption. Among those branches, there was one gap ; and Father d'Alzon's successor, Father Picard, completed the Assumptionist family by the founding of *Les Orantes de l'Assomption*, literally and pre-eminently, " the praying Sisters of the Assumption "—the all-important contemplative heart of the whole ideal. The Foundress was Isabelle de Clermont-Tonnerre comtesse d'Ursel, who became Mother Isabelle-Marie of Gethsemani. But closely associated with her in the foundation was the Oblate, Mother Marie of the Compassion, whom Father Picard had summoned from Nîmes to be the Superior and Mother of the first *Orantes*. " In recounting the story of our beginnings," writes one of these first Sisters, " it is difficult to find words to express the sweetness and fraternal affection which united the two Sisters : the Oblate and the *Orante*." Mother Marie brought a clear head and a warm heart to her work. Father Picard chose very well ; for, with her great experience of the science of prayer, she had a born genius for forming souls, with a firm gentleness and a gentle firmness, to the life of contemplation. Her name is lovingly remembered among the *Orantes*, for through her another historical connection was made between the branches of the Assumption : Father Picard, the Assumptionist priest, Mother Isabelle the *Orante*, and Mother Marie the Oblate, stand together in that great moment when the contemplative heart of the Assumption became a resplendent reality.

When her task with the *Orantes* was finished, she turned, in a spirit of complete adaptability, to her new task—which included the making of worsted blankets to eke out the poverty of the Oblate pioneers in Charlton. In thus turning from the exalted and sublime task of training souls, to the humdrum task she was now performing with the same zeal and self-dedication, she made the pattern of her life a magnificent example of the Oblate of the Assumption. She did not live to see the fruits of that spirit in the fine development that was to take place in Charlton. She had valiantly performed her hard task of laying the all important spiritual foundations ; and they were solidly laid, for they were laid with intense prayer. " Foundations ", as Wordsworth said in one of his inspired moments, " must be laid in heaven ".

THE SPIRIT OF THE OBLATES

WHEN Father d'Alzon searched for an image which would bring home to his Oblates what their animating spirit should be, he chose that scriptural picture of Saul lifting his sightless eyes to the mysterious power which had struck down his body into the dust of the Damascene road and his spirit into the dust of its own nothingness, while the new voice of Paul vibrant with the future spoke a brave surrender : "Lord, what wouldst Thou have me to do ? " In the heart of the whole Assumptionist ideal is the universal rallying cry : *Adveniat Regnum Tuum* ; but that ideal has given birth to many families within the Assumptionist Group, and each family has its own motto voicing the special manner in which each realizes that ideal. The Oblate Sister of the Assumption has been given a motto—an ideal of service—which takes her back to that brave moment on the Road to Damascus when Paul reached groping hands before him, seeking the Will of God ; and to that mystery-filled moment when an archangel heard a girl change the whole course of history with the words : " Behold the handmaid of the Lord, be it done unto me according to Thy word." *Ecce*, said Mary ; *Ecce Ego* comes the answering voice of the Oblate, who lifts her eyes to Mary as her model. *Ecce Ego, Mitte Me !*—Here I am, Send Me !—is the motto of the Oblates, which catches in a few words the distinguishing trait of this Congregation born of the full maturity of Emmanuel d'Alzon. It is the mind of St. Paul when he flung wide all his powers, all his enthusiasm, and asked only that the way should be pointed out to him. The words of this motto were the inspiration of Isaias when, afire with contemplation of God's infinite magnitude, he turned eagerly to seek any form of work which would further His Kingdom on earth.

This spirit of complete adaptability, of unrestricted pliability to any and every need of the Church, has a field of action whose only limits are the needs of the Church. It is a spirit which incarnates itself immediately in a true missionary vocation. Every apostolic undertaking, as well as every attempt to increase in personal holiness, is impregnated with this spirit. Because of the historical circumstances which attended their foundation and directed their activities, from their birth to the missions of the Near East, their aim was the very definite and very exacting one of striving for the return of dissident Christians to the love of Christ and the unity of the Church. The point to be remembered about all this is that these ideas were not laid down in the cold abstract like mathematical symbols scraped in the sand with a piece of dry bone. They welled up from the living soul of Emmanuel d'Alzon, warm with his blood, alive with his vision, instinct with that *Catholicity* which he felt all around in Rome, when he was working so diligently in connection with the Vatican Council and the Definition of Papal Infallibility. It has been said that Rome dwarfs a man. It did not dwarf Emmanuel d'Alzon, but lifted him to the full poetic height of his own ideals and ideas, by showing him, in vital fashion, how all those ideals and ideas would bear the fruit he sought from them only if they were made one with the living Mystical Body of Christ, the living and life-giving Church. His was no abstract enthusiasm, dry as a phrase from Canon Law. Truth ran to a sort of deep poetry in the soul of Emmanuel d'Alzon, and coursed wildly in his veins ; and it was with all the warmth and urgency of his nature that, in the midst of those heaped-up labours which made his energy so talked of in Rome, that he poured out his ideas in letter after letter to Mother Emmanuel-Marie Correnson and to his Daughters. There is nothing stale or stilted about these letters, nor about any of his letters. How refreshing it is, for example, to come on the expletive : " *What vile ink !* " bracketed in the middle of a sentence ; or this : " *I have just posted a letter to Father Em-* (*interrupted by Abbé Chesnel*) *-manuel* . . ." Letter came on the heels of letter from Father d'Alzon to his beloved Oblates, and in every letter—written in that headlong handwriting of his, sloping upwards and suggesting to Father Galeran (*Croquis*) " the course of a mettlesome horse rushing up a steep incline, its flanks ceaselessly whipped by an eager rider "—he reiterated his ideas for his Oblates and his burning desire for their personal holiness so that each might become in her own life a holocaust of oblation for the extension of the Kingdom of God. It was as a synthesis of these ideas that Father Cornillie A. A., in his fine *L'Oblate de l'Assomption*, defined an Oblate as " a soul naturally sacrificed in humility ". Father Emmanuel Bailly, of the Assumption, gave this splendid description :

" The Oblate is a soul offered in oblation, in perpetual sacrifice, lifting up to God the Father her life, her sacrifices, her obedience, her self-abnegation, her helplessness, her humiliations . . . for the saving of souls. Her whole life is consumed as a holocaust for those who make no expiation, who offer no satisfaction, and she endeavours to supply to her Heavenly Father a superabundance of expiation for herself and for others. You are called to be victims, but victims of love, for such is your vocation ".

And again, Father Picard, Second Superior General of the Oblates, stressed the same idea as the ascetical and mystical stamp of the Oblates' spirituality : " Offer yourselves as victims. Let the spirit of expiation take deep root in you . . ."

Before turning to the letters and writings of Father d'Alzon to see how ardently he inculcated this idea seized on by his disciples Bailly and Picard as the essence of the Oblate spirit, it is as well to establish what we mean by the " spirit " of a Religious Order or Congregation. The word " spirit " is here an analogy with the idea of " soul "—the life-principle which animates the body. We may therefore accept as adequate, a certain theologian's definition of the " spirit " of an order as " the characteristic and permanent way of feeling, of knowing and of willing, which the tradition of the Order reveals and which is exemplified in its members ". Father d'Alzon mysteriously knew, in 1870, that he had only ten years to live, and he laboured passionately to establish that spirit—that " way of feeling, knowing and willing "—firmly in his Oblates. " *I am sometimes convinced* " he wrote to Mother Emmanuel-Marie of the Compassion from Rome, " *that God will give me ten years more of life, my last ten years from sixty to seventy ; and that, just as Our Lord did His external work for three years and three months, even so will He give me three times that amount of time to perform our work.*" The reading of his letters dating from that time leaves no doubt that he passionately regarded this last great work of his life as the crown of his ideal. When he was in Rome, many things reminded him of his Oblates :

"*You know, it is awe-inspiring to say Mass every day in the room where Saint Catherine of Sienna died. Does it not make one wish to have only Saint Catherines as Daughters, for you know that she wasn't exactly an effeminate person.*" That Father d'Alzon should have held up the example of the virile Catherine to his Daughters, is very natural indeed, for he himself wrote to Marie Correnson : "*Yes, Marie, I no longer wish you to be a woman, I want you to be a man.*"

Also, there is this delightful touch : "*I pause to tell you that at this very moment I can hear a clock which has the very same chime as that which in (Nîmes) Cathedral announces the Lenten Sermons. Alas ! I am far from that poor Cathedral, and from my Daughters who can hear the sound of its bells. As to the chimes, I sacrifice them willingly ; but what of my Daughters ? Yes, I commend them to God, and my sacrifice is all the more meritorious because it is hard.*"

Again it was to his Oblates that he looked for spiritual help : "*It is very true that I count on no branch of the Assumptionist family as I do on the Oblates of Nîmes and Le Vigan, to do violence to Our Lord on my behalf*" . . . And always, always, there is that intense concern with the spiritual development, the spiritual quality of Mother Emmanuel-Marie and her Daughters.

The idea which Father d'Alzon wished to breathe incessantly into the soul of every Oblate, so as to give the distinctive Oblate "colouring" to her whole personality and become the source of her spiritual élan, is *immolation.* "*I want you*", he writes, "*to make a firm resolution of becoming real victims of love for the salvation of souls.*" He shows his Daughters how this self-immolation is the source of that missionary apostolicity which is the key-note to their whole vocation. For apostolicity means devotion to the cause of the spread of Christ's Kingdom, and that devotion is effective only to the extent to which it is unmixed with self-love and self-seeking. The supreme Image of supreme selfless sacrifice is the Image of Christ on Calvary, and it is to that Image that Father d'Alzon recalls his Daughters again and again, in order to animate their gift of self to the point of heroism. " *The soul must do its part* ", he writes, " *by bearing the Cross of Christ, by following Christ to Calvary. Let the placing of the cross on the shoulders of Christ be for us a very hard, but a very practical lesson. . . . Do we wish to put ourselves beyond the reach of all error? Let us go and question the Cross, and act on the answers It gives us* " . . .

Their greatest glory—and his—would be if their lives were to end on Calvary through martyrdom for the Faith : " *Yes, indeed, my very dear Daughters, I would be enchanted if some day the instruments of your torture were brought to me, or your habits coloured with your blood.*"

He flings great horizons of missionary endeavour before them, that they may raise their eyes to them and never drop their gaze again to the petty preoccupations of the self : " *Here I am again to tell you how much my mind is occupied with all the work which we could do for the Church if we really aimed at being valiant soldiers. The field is immense . . . Thus, behind the Bulgarians, you have the great mass of schismatic Slavs of whom the Bulgarians are only a branch. You have at least sixty millions to convert—no less ! Ah, if we had the hearts of seraphim and of apostles, what great inroads would we not make there and in many other places !* "

We notice here that he brings together the idea of *seraphim* and *apostle* ; for he was very insistent on the part played by chastity, and by that strange power that lives in chastity, in engendering dynamic apostolicity. It was said of Emmanuel d'Alzon by those who wished to express supreme admiration of him, that he was " a virginal soul." He himself knew the power that goes out from purity, and he endeavours to instil that same power into his Daughters.

" *In my adoration of the Blessed Sacrament* ", he writes in the *Directory* he gave them, " *I shall ask my Divine Saviour to inebriate me with the wine that brings forth virgins, and I shall ask the holy angels who surround His throne to make my soul and my heart as pure as theirs* " . . . Chastity is power, because power is union with Christ in the immolation of self, and chastity accentuates the image of God in the soul. The distance between us and Infinite Purity is lessened : " *It is one of the great effects of God's mercy* ", writes Father d'Alzon, " *that without changing our nature which He*

*created and which implies in us the indissoluble union of soul and of body,
we can nevertheless always aim, by His grace, at approaching nearer to
His infinite purity* " . . . Here, again, the emphasis is on immolation, for impurity is egoism, and egoism fixes the eyes on the
little circle of self-interest. The apostle must be spiritually
free, and it is the eternal paradox for the wisdom of the flesh,
that those only are supremely free who have bound themselves
with the fetters of Poverty, Obedience and Chastity. " *Develop
the empire of the spirit* ", writes Father d'Alzon, " *that is to say,
the action of God within you, and you develop in yourself—immortality.
. . .*" " *Ask for sacrifice from a soul : the more that soul is pure, the
more it is free to make that sacrifice, because no earthly bond holds it
captive*" . . . " *Where chastity reigns, the spirit of sacrifice develops ; where
chastity is shipwrecked, vocations disappear* " . . . And finally, there
is this fine passage from his *Meditation on Religious Perfection :*

" *Who are these virgins who love Him whose name is as oil which
penetrates sweetly . . . if not these virginal souls who, enchanted with
the beauty of the Saviour, allow themselves to be penetrated by His
secret, silent, powerful action, producing wonders of perfection ? . . . A
certain freshness of soul is necessary in order to draw nearer to Christ,
and He Himself preserves that freshness when the soul delivers itself
without reserve to the action of His power, and even when a soul,
having withdrawn from his empire, seriously desires to return* " . . .
This " freshness " is the great source of apostolicity, and " the
apostle," he writes, " *ought to become as an angel, having snapped the
bonds of the flesh in order to accomplish more rapidly the missions which
have been given to him . . . My life ought to be every day more and more
spiritual, in order that it may be more angelic, more divine, in a more
perfect imitation of Christ . . .* The chastity of the apostle is
expiatory chastity, and, he goes on, " *this great mystery of expiation, so intimately linked with the mystery of the Communion of Saints,
implies, by charity, my obligation to combat the tyranny of the flesh, first
of all in myself, then in others, by a mortification like to that of Our
Lord. By the destruction of the domination of the flesh, we are able to
work for the extension of God's Kingdom in ourselves, in the
Church, among sinners, and thus to broaden the kingdom of the saints* "
. . . Thus too, no matter at what point one enters into the
doctrine he laid down for his Daughters, the wheel of Father

d'Alzon's thought comes full circle to the master idea of immolation and selflessness. The definition of an Oblate remains the same, no matter what aspect of her work or her spirituality is considered : *Vie d'Oblate, vie d'oblation* (The life of an Oblate, a life of oblation) as yet another of Father d'Alzon's successors has put it.

The special stamp by which Father d'Alzon would have men know that they are Oblates of the Assumption, is their Catholicity and their devotion to the Holy See. In a letter from Rome in 1870, he lays down as one of the conditions of their future development : " *Love of the Church. This arises very specially for you, both from your vocation and from present circumstances. You must be in a very special way the workers of the Church, and, at the same time, you ought to consider that, since you are privileged to live during the holding of a Council, you must prepare yourselves to profit by all the graces which will result from it for true Christians. Remember that you are destined to make that Church loved to which God has confided the salvation of the world*" . . . He calls on Mother Emmanuel-Marie to enter into his feelings about what is happening in Rome, and thereby to appreciate just how necessary the spirit he is cultivating in her and in her daughters has come to be.

Rome, 20th March, 1870.

" *I wrote to you yesterday, my dear child, and I take up my pen again to-day that you may share something of what I am suffering in being witness to certain human, too human, intrigues to paralyse the Council. The Council will be one of the most mediocre which we have had, if I consider the way in which attempts are being made to lessen it. The people who are making these attempts do not see that humanity is before the bishops, like a patient who can be saved only by a painful operation ; but the patient cries aloud, and the sanctimonious and stupid compassion of the doctors suspends the operation, applies a cataplasm and allows the wound to grow gangrenous and the patient to die. The Church will not die ; but where will human grace descend? I ask myself what will be the state of things in a few years, when the liberal heresy will have made its nest, or rather, will have profited by the fissures through which the imbecility of certain people would allow it to escape under pretext of charity. Also I am sometimes convinced that God, choosing what is most feeble to confound what is most strong, wills to give a magnificent mission to the Oblates.*

This depends on you, if setting aside a host of petty annoyances, you use your utmost endeavour to give to your Daughters the full sweep, the whole breadth of the Catholic spirit. You must be a daughter of the Catholic Church. This must be your single great concern, and you must bend all your efforts towards achieving this. A mighty intellect is not needed here, but you must have an immense spirit of faith, and you must communicate that spirit to your Daughters. Speak to them often about the Church; read, as much as your health allows, literature which deals with the Church and which helps you to see how beautiful it is to serve, before all else, the cause of our Lord and of His Church. I am continually occupied with endeavouring to see what we can accomplish in this connection . . ."

He calls, therefore, on his Daughters to serve the Church with every fibre of their being, and the vision of that Church which he holds up before the chaste eyes of their souls is living beauty —not a dry abstraction, but the extension of the personality and power of Christ into space and time. The source of the Oblate's love for the Church is her own personal love for Christ, which makes her love the things that Christ loved, and therefore supremely love the Church "born of His death" and the object of His Love . . . "*He descended from Heaven*", writes Father d'Alzon in the *Directory*, "*He became man, He was born in a stable, He passed thirty years in the labours of a hard, poor and hidden life. He suffered calumnies, insults, persecutions, the most awful sufferings, and death on the Cross. All this was for His Church, His Mystical Body.*" . . . All this "emptying" of Himself, all these humiliations and sufferings, issued with His death in something very beautiful—His Church, the "new Jerusalem." . . ."*Her purple robe is stained with the blood of her sons*", writes Father d'Alzon, "*and she is ready, as a bride adorned for her bridegroom, because she knows how to deck herself out in the finery that best becomes her*" . . . When he writes to Mother Emmanuel-Marie from Rome, he speaks of the Church as a woman in labour, and his words are full of that deep personal concern of a man who here thinks with his heart:

"*At this moment, the Catholic world is certainly filled with a heavy sense of expectancy, which certain opposing elements would change to anguish. But the Church, like a woman, must suffer when it gives birth, because every creature is in that childbirth and that pain . . . You see, my child, that as I write I am weighed down with heavy concern, and I allow that concern to overflow into your heart. For your part, you must pray, you must ask, you must do violence to God, you must compel the Spirit of Love to suffuse the earth with truth . . ."*

Through his *Directory*, he gives the Church to his Oblates as their fatherland. " *The Church is the* patria—*the fatherland—of my soul, the society through which I am united with God.*" They were to go forth among many nations to bear the standard of Christ ; that standard was the Cross, and not the flag of any local patriotism. In a very salutary lesson indeed, he pointed out how the Church and the seamless garment of its truth were never to be degraded to the service of anything less than the sanctification of souls and the things of the Spirit. " *Would you credit that I no longer feel urged to concern myself with the Poles ? This is not because I am unaware that they are such sad victims indeed of Russian tyranny, but because they are using the Catholic Church as a weapon against 'russification'. If, like the Irish, they had regarded themselves as Catholics before all else, then that would be a different matter. But their plan of campaign is to use Catholicism to defend 'polandism'* " . . . So, by example, precept, and ceaseless urging, Father d'Alzon stamped his Oblates with that devotion to the Church and to Rome which is one of their marked characteristics to-day.

As would be naturally expected, the type of piety which Father d'Alzon inculcated with all this, was essentially liturgical and absolutely masculine. " *Avoid singularity and exaggeration* ", he advises his disciples—and it was the same spiritual training which he gave to his Sisters : " *Do not be at the mercy of every whim, but always keep an even keel . . . Let there be no spiritual wry-neck in your piety, nor any showing of the whites of your eyes to the angels when you pray, meditate, or contemplate . . . Before all else, love the devotions of the Church, which you should prefer to devotional practices which are the product of pious fantasy. Love the liturgy, plain chant and the divine Office . . .*" He constantly insisted on the necessity for truly Catholic piety—disinterested, generous, universal, the the product in fact of that selfless *immolation* which he laid down as the essence of the Oblate's holiness. He would have them cultivate in their piety as in their virtues " *the full sweep, the whole breadth of the Catholic spirit* ". The key-stone of their piety is the Divine Office, the Hours of which they recite every day, Matins being reserved for the principal Feasts of the liturgical year. " *The Office on earth* ", reads the Directory, " *is the function of the angels in Heaven, praising God with the inspirations of God* " . . . " *When I recite the Office, I must enter into all the intentions of the Church, that society of Saints paying its debt to God, and asking for the perseverance of the just and the conversion of sinners.*"

All this builds up to a magnificent ideal of selfless service of the Church, with liturgical prayer as its very breath, the whole being diffused with radiant love for God and the Blessed Mother of God—Our Lady of the Assumption. The Oblate's life of union is to be deeply nourished by prayer, and therefore she must know how to avoid the danger of false emotional pietism by meditating " *not only on points of piety, but on dogmatic truths which yield results most fruitful for true perfection, even if they are not the most sentimental* ". (Supplement to *Directory*.) The Oblate, if she is to be a " *living copy of the Divine Saviour and not just a chimera* ", must study Christ in His Mysteries, in order that she may absorb the spirit of Christ and reproduce it in her own life. There is something of the spirit of Berulle about the manner in which Father d'Alzon stresses the contemplation of the ' states ' of Christ in the spirituality of his Oblates. " *You see* ", he writes (Sup. Dir.), " *all the mysteries of the life of Christ opening out before you. There are the details of His life as a man, and each of these details embodies a virtue* . . . *The infinite unity of God seems too mysterious for our weakness ; yet here are details, and divine details, and there is not a corner of our lives that cannot be penetrated by them. Jesus Christ, the perfect man, is always before us in His mysteries. Know Him then ever more intimately, imitate Him more and more divinely* " . . . One feels that it is with the enthusiasm of a Berulle that Father d'Alzon would have his Daughters to approach those mysteries of Christ ; for with what enthusiasm he himself must have come on such a passage as this one from Berulle on the Incarnation—a veritable prose-poem : " Now light leaps from highest heaven to deepest earth, without defilement ; it penetrates

Father Picard, thus bringing into existence a second Congregation of Oblates with Paris as its centre.

We have used the word " schism " here—but let us hasten to blunt the sharp associations of the word by adding that there was only a material divergence, never a divergence of heart and mind, between the two groups.   It was, we repeat, a clash of sincerities between two deeply sincere persons who had fundamentally the same mind ; and that sincerity lived on.   A clear proof of this is the fact that, in our choice of individual Sisters as embodiments of the Oblate ideal, we have been able to draw equally on both groups.   Both branches preserved intact the spirit breathed on them by Father d'Alzon, and both branches yearned for unity. As a result of this unity-in-schism, a remarkable thing happened, which is surely the whole reason for detailing this history. When, as a result of continued efforts the schism was healed in 1926, the two groups merged easily, and no readjustment was found necessary.   It was a moment of great rejoicing for both.

The Foundress had died surrounded by her Sisters, on July 24th, 1900. How intensely, but with what resignation and purity of vision, she suffered as a result of this schism ; and also as a result of the final thorn in her crown—her removal from her position as Superior, while retaining the name of Foundress— belong to the story of Marie Correnson.

APPENDIX TWO

ONE OF THE illustrations included in this book gives a sample of the handwriting of Father d'Alzon in his late sixties. There is a dash and vigour in it—" the course of a mettlesome horse rushing up a steep incline "—which bespeaks the undiminished energy of the man himself. What it says is equally eloquent of a man on whose ideals the dust of age could never settle : *Suffering for the Love of Christ.*

" I shall show him all that he must suffer for my name's sake " (Acts of the Apostles). This name which must be carried to the ends of the earth, must be so carried through suffering. Thus you have been warned that you must suffer much, endure all, in order to be an Oblate, a Virgin-Apostle. Do you realize what that word implies ? St. Teresa says : Either to suffer or to die. St. Magdalen de Pazzi, if I am not mistaken, puts it more emphatically : Always to suffer, never to die. Why ? Because when one dies, one goes to heaven ; but the Kingdom of God is no longer proclaimed by us, and it must be proclaimed in spite of all obstacles.

(Extract from the retreat preached to the Oblates of the Assumption : September, 1876. Third Instruction : *Of the particular purpose of the Oblate's Vocation—a missionary Vocation.*)